D1271850

The
Traveling
Man

By Truman E. Moore

THE TRAVELING MAN
THE SLAVES WE RENT

The
TRAVELING
MAN

The Story of the
American Traveling Salesman

———

by

Truman E. Moore

———

Doubleday & Company, Inc.
Garden City, New York, 1972

ISBN: 0-385-01351-5
Library of Congress Catalog Card Number 71-150907
Copyright © 1972 by Truman E. Moore
All Rights Reserved
Printed in the United States of America
First Edition

CONTENTS

INTRODUCTION

The image of the traveling salesman has faded until he has become the ghost of commerce past, slipping out of the consciousness of modern man. Traveling salesman . . . we think of old jokes, of Willy Loman in *Death of a Salesman*, Hickey in *The Iceman Cometh*, or Harold Hill in *The Music Man*. We reach back, groping vaguely in our minds for some point in time bounded by innocence, wonder, nostalgia, and pity. When the sales manager rises at the end of the annual sales dinner and taps his water glass for attention, it is an even bet that he will pay homage to one of these images and he will do it in hurt and angry tones, denying that the bent figure of a tired man, a wrinkled suit, a worn sample case, and a pained and anxious ego are part of being a salesman today. We aren't like that any more, he says. The world has changed and we salesmen have changed with it. People only think of us as we used to be. These are modern times and we are modern men.

This book is an attempt to follow the life of the traveling man, through his first days as a peddler, his triumph as a dandy drummer, and his transformation into a unit of production. His history and development parallel the history of America, and perhaps by watching what happened to him, we might catch sight of what happened to all of us.

for Rebecca

Chapter One

Fleece and Fly in the Colonies

The prototype of the American traveling salesman was the peddler who wandered through the roadless countryside or poled a raft down the smooth, broad rivers in the late 1600s, carrying small items to sell or trade to the families in remote settlements in New England and the South. Peddlers also traded among the Indians, as did the fur trappers, and the first factory built in America made glass beads for the Indian trade.

The first peddlers were from Boston. They were young men of families without money or influence, who found no future for themselves in the confines of colonial society, although there were exceptions—adventurous lads from substantial families, like Bronson Alcott, later to be father of transcendentalism and Louisa Mae. He was as deep into what Chevalier called the American penchant for *le make-money* as any of the tough, haggling young Yankees who lived by "fleece and fly." His biographer treats the commercial side of Alcott's nature quite fully in *Pedlar's Progress*.[1]

In colonial New England, unless a man owned property valued at 200 pounds, his vocational choice was limited to the trades. Only a "freeman" could be a merchant, enter law, the clergy, or medicine, wear fine clothes, and be called "mister." Otherwise, he was a "goodman" and he could go to sea, fish, work in the shipyards, or spend seven years as an unpaid apprentice to a tradesman. To many lads, these choices were not appealing.

Boston Harbor was a bustling place of action, and here a goodman who wanted to become a peddler bargained for pins, needles, thread, lace, buttons, spices, various items of hardware, combs, razors, and scissors smuggled ashore in the pockets of sailors or sold in the small shops of importers along the bay.

Much of what went into the peddler's pack was contraband, thereby tainting American commerce with the stigma of illicit origin. Smuggling was the general practice, and the brisk coastal trade that developed between New England and the South was illegal. The seafaring peddlers and off-season fishermen loaded coasting shallops and ketches with contraband from the wharves of Salem, Boston, New Haven, and New York, and traded along the waterways of the Chesapeake, and into Virginia and the Carolinas, for tobacco that by law was to be sold only to England. Attempts to stop these boat peddlers by levying high customs fees set off a rebellion in the Carolinas in 1676.

Not all the early traveling salesmen were peddlers or off-season fishermen. Many ship captains took cargoes to distant ports and personally sold the goods for what they could get. One captain rented a building in Lima, Peru, stocked it with his cargo, and ran a store for almost a year before returning home. "By 1665, more than 300 New England-owned vessels were sailing in the trade with the West Indies and Europe. By 1717, better than 200 vessels sailed annually from New York with export cargo, and about as many cleared from Philadelphia." These captains were "among the first American salesmen."[2] Their adventures have never been fully appreciated in the telling of American history.

The American Revolution interrupted the peddler's smuggling trade, but those who managed to avoid the interruption did well. There was, in fact, a lot of business to interrupt, which was one of the causes of the Revolution. Business was good, and the English kept getting in the way. The colonies could never have paid all the duties and levies imposed on them had they not earned the money by smuggling. Over a fourth of the signers of the Declaration of Independence were smugglers, and indeed John Hancock was called the "prince of smugglers." A third of the trade in New York and Boston was illegal, and thirty to forty thousand smugglers operated on the English Coast.

According to Malcomb Keir, who edited a comprehensive history of New England manufacturing, it was not the seafaring peddler who had the greatest influence on American manufacturing, but the pack peddler, traveling on foot, on horseback, and later, when there were more roads, by wagon. Big-city storekeepers preferred to carry English-made goods, claiming that they were superior to domestic products. The pack peddlers carried American-made products to the hinterlands and sold them to farmers and townspeople who didn't mind native goods. The hardware industry, in particular, is indebted to the peddler for its survival in those early days.

In Europe, by the way, the presence of peddlers was rare, due to the craft guilds that provided local artisans with a monopoly in their territory. Little business was allowed the European peddler. In America, the situation was quite different, with a shortage of craftsmen and a weak or nonexistent guild system outside the major towns. Villages and settlements were springing up

every year, offering a market to anyone able to supply
the goods.

By the beginning of the eighteenth century, the
New England peddler was traveling all over the West
and South. Peddling was already recognized as a way to
wealth, and sons of peddlers were rising into the merchant class. Richardson Wright, author of one of the
best books about this period, cites a visitor to Boston in
1699 who observed that "in the chief of High Street
there are stately edifices, some of which cost the owners
two or three thousand pounds the raising . . . for the
fathers of these men were tinkers and peddlers."[3]

In 1740, the arrival in Berlin, Connecticut, of two
Irish tinsmiths started the transformation of the random
wandering of the Yankee peddlers into something resembling a sales force for American industry, then in
its infant years.

A great tinware boom was set off by Edgar and
William Pattison, who emigrated from County Tyrone in
1738.

The colonial household was not a place of great
adornment. Purchases were few and limited to necessities,
though many a farmer's wife must have longed for a
bit of finery. The silver-bright gleam of tin pots and pans
tapped the unsuspected reservoirs of pent-up colonial
consumer demand. Most housewives were eager to have
this gleaming replacement for their dull and dented
pewter, although it was not popular at the higher levels
of society. When a tavernkeeper set George Washington's
table with tin utensils, the General sent a boy over to
the home of a local judge to borrow some silverware
for the meal. Fortunately for tin peddlers, Virginia aristo-
crats did not comprise a large part of the potential
market.

Tinware was no innovation. Indian traders had
swapped tin dishes for furs as early as 1584. Its subsequent absence from the American table ended when the

Pattisons, by accident or design, discovered the market. The traveling salesman has often been called a civilizing influence because he carried the latest products and newest inventions to the far reaches of the world. The benefits to civilization from tinware may not have been great, but in the hands of the peddlers, tinware appeared on the tables of the remotest cabin, and no trail was left untrod.

The Pattisons' shop in Berlin, Connecticut, produced various tin items—plates, cups, spoons, forks, pans, pitchers, and pails. They peddled their stock around town and then retired to the shop to make more. The business prospered and they found it necessary to hire apprentices and peddlers to cover Connecticut and the surrounding colonies. Tin peddlers were soon making regular trips into the South and West. Other tinware shops opened, and for the next hundred years Berlin was the center of the tinware business. After its decline, the region remained a center for the metal and hardware industry, as it is today.

The growth of peddling as a business encountered one serious difficulty. By the nineteenth century, most states had laws either licensing or restricting peddlers.

The storekeepers, many of whom were themselves former peddlers, watched the passing parade of Yankee peddlers with growing resentment. Feeling that their domain was being invaded, the local merchants began to assert their territorial imperative by bringing pressure on the legislature for laws against peddling. A series of fines and restrictions against peddlers in Rhode Island finally culminated in 1728 in an outright ban on peddling. Pennsylvania began to license peddlers, and Connecticut—the great source of most of the commercial wanderers—placed a heavy tax on goods brought into the state. Connecticut merchants petitioned the government to ban all peddlers from entry because "they carried contagious diseases." Presumably, Connecticut peddlers were immune to infection.

Years later, after time and progress had made the peddler obsolete, the laws remained on the books, and the feeling against the intrusion of outsiders remained unshaken. Traveling salesmen on the road before the Civil War were fined and jailed with the old peddler laws or with new laws against salesmen who carried samples. On the outskirts of many small towns today are signs declaring "No peddling or soliciting," though the ordinance is often unenforced.

The trickle of peddlers that annoyed merchants and storekeepers grew to a steadier stream each year despite prohibitive laws. It was perhaps his uncertain standing with the law and his popularity with his customers that gave the peddler an ambivalent status borne by salesmen ever since.

In order to circumvent the antipeddler laws, which proliferated along the Eastern Seaboard, the tinsmiths set up shops and warehouses in the southern and midwestern states. In so doing, the peddler could rightfully claim that his product was of local manufacture and gain immunity from legal harassment. Later, the clock peddlers used the same procedure, setting up assembly shops in the South, where clocks were simply put together and adjusted. It pleased local residents to think that such complicated mechanisms were being made in their own state.

The supply routes thus established—with warehouses and distribution points—became the framework for the wholesale and retail trade of today.

The number of peddlers on the road grew constantly. In good times the stories of success told by returning peddlers attracted others to take up the pack. In bad times the lack of opportunity at home forced many young men to try their hand at peddling.

During the Revolution there was the usual amount

of wartime profiteering by wholesalers, big merchants, little storekeepers, and Yankee peddlers. Unfortunately, the peddler was made the most frequent object of the patriot's outrage. Complaints were heard that peddlers and "persons no one ever heard of" had "risen to affluence and were usurping the places of the old families."[4] Upward mobility was not yet appreciated, as we can clearly see by the reactions of an officer of the Continental Army who encountered four travelers on the road, all wearing uniforms resplendent with swords and cockades. They stopped at an inn, where six other similarly dressed fellows joined them. The officer supposed them to be soldiers and was shocked to learn that they were "itinerant traders" who boasted of the fabulous sums they made selling and trading from town to town.

Returning home to his own farm, the officer discovered that his hired man had quit to become a peddler, and no amount of pleading or threatening could get him back. The former hired man offered instead to buy his master's Army coat, complaining that he lacked a proper one befitting his new occupation. The indignant officer retired to the Golden Ball Tavern—by the fireside, I imagine, and with a mug of rum flip at his elbow—and penned a letter to the editor of the Hartford *Courant*, and thus left his observations and his outrage to history.

Merchants pursued their business with great enthusiasm and apparent disregard for the outcome of the Revolution. A Boston firm was appointed Collectors of Clothing for the Army, which resulted in lucrative contracts for them. In 1778, while "they were figuring whether they should make one or two hundred percent out of the soldiers' winter clothing . . . the soldiers themselves . . . shivering and naked at Valley Forge, [were] dying of cold and starvation."[5]

If there seemed to be little public outcry against such fraud, it was probably because it was unknown. Merchants did not go about in contrived costumes,

boasting of their profits in every tavern and coaching
house.

The number of peddlers on the road by the end of
the Revolution had fallen to a handful, but after the war
ended there were more peddlers than ever. Before 1776,
most colonists stayed at home and lived quiet, unevent-
ful lives. Now these men who had marched about in the
war saw the peddler's life on the road in a new light.
Restless young men who were unwilling to go back to
the simple life on the farm, filled a peddler's pack and
set out to make a fortune. Some did. Most had a few
vagabond years before finding a place to settle down,
wiser, and perhaps richer, for the experience.

The Yankee tin peddler became a familiar sight all
over the country. The peddler carried his tinware in
two trunks slung over his shoulder as he started down the
trail. Staggering under the weight of a hundred pounds
of tinware and notions, faced with the prospect of marches
longer and more burdened than any he ever made in
the Army, the young peddler must have recalled his
old place at the plow or the apprentice's bench with
fond nostalgia and some regret.

After the Revolution, manufactured goods from
abroad were again plentiful, and this abundance was
added to by the growing industries of New England.
There was, however, a shortage of money following the
disgrace of the Continental dollar. Prices dropped sharply.
I like to think that in the inexorable grinding of economic
law, the plumed peddlers and greedy merchants received
their just rewards.

Economic stability had returned by 1790, and the
peddlers' prosperity was supplemented unexpectedly by
Jefferson's embargo of American ports in an effort to
stay out of further trouble with England.

The Connecticut *Courant* called it the Dambargo,
and wailed that "the little finger of Thomas Jefferson
[is] heavier than the loins of George the Third."

Unpopular with the New England shipping interests and the rural South, the embargo nurtured the growth of domestic industry, much of which relied heavily, and some exclusively, on the peddler for distribution, sales, and advertising. Even after the Revolution, Americans still preferred British goods, and Yankee manufacturers were forced to sell through peddlers.

Unexpected aid for the peddlers came as the result of a prize piece of British folly. At the end of the War of 1812, English manufacturers, alarmed at the persistent growth of American industry, decided to simply put it out of business. Their plan was to undersell American industry to death. American wholesalers watched shiploads of British goods dumped onto the American market at prices representing only a small fraction of their true worth. The American importers went on one of the greatest bargain sprees in history.

Crates of the best English pewter were sold on the pier as soon as they were landed. Case after case of genuine Sheffield silver was snapped up by the importers and before nightfall was being readily sold into the surrounding homes by peddlers. Tons of the finest tools from Birmingham were on their way into our Middle West as fast as wagons could carry them. Locks and keys, nails and screws, razors and scissors poured into our ports and were sold for whatever they would bring . . .[6]

For almost a year, British industry flooded American markets with underpriced goods. Peddlers in the port cities crammed their packs with fine goods and headed for the back country. 1815 was the year of the Great Peddler Windfall, and American industry may thank the peddler for his energy. By the end of the year, the English felt the American market was a bottomless pit, and they ceased their expensive methods of trying to fill it.

Industries sprouted all over New England, and there was more for the peddler to sell now than tinware and odds and ends.

To encourage manufacturing, monopolies had been granted for a specified time. Thomas Darling of New Haven, for example, was granted the exclusive right to make window glass for twenty years, "provided he made 500 feet in every four years."[7]

Sometimes with special grants, often in direct competition, industry began to grow. Brass buttons, buckles, and silver pewter came out of Waterbury, and here the brass industry would flourish in the years to come, just as the manufacture of hardware had grown from the Berlin tinware shops. Eli Terry had started making wooden clocks by hand, "and a few daring proprietors of struggling cotton, silk, wool and paper mills were establishing . . . the feeble forerunners of the great brass, cotton, silk and woolen mills of today. They were especially significant because of their influence in localizing later industrial centers."[8] Most recently we have seen rapid growth of the electronics industry in New England as a result of its industrial capacity, although the Yankee peddler's part in this development has been forgotten.

The bulk of the manufacture was still tinware and "Yankee notions" for the peddlers, which, "like the theme of an opera (*Il Trovatore*, no doubt), underlies the great romance of the Connecticut metal industry,"[9] as one historian so imaginatively put it.

Between 1808 and 1815, helped by the extreme protection of Mr. Jefferson's Dambargo, and the British blockades before and during the War of 1812, the brass and hardware industries, clock factories, mills, and plants of every sort sprang up beside the streams of the Naugatuck Valley, of which Waterbury was the center. Elsewhere in New England the growth was as rapid. Eli Whitney introduced the factory system by the use of interchangeable parts, and did for manufacturing what his cotton gin had done for agriculture. It is doubtful that any other man had more impact upon American industry than did this Yankee genius.

At first, the pack peddler had brought only the small luxuries and necessities to the cabin door. The tin peddler added more things to his pack, and he prospered and got a horse. The demand for goods and supplies grew with the country. The river towns couldn't get large quantities of supplies to the inland settlements without roads, and the peddler could only carry so much on his back or in his saddlebags. From both the peddlers and the settlers the cry went up for roads, and between 1790 and 1840, America began road-building on a scale not equaled until recent times.

Many of the roads built during this era were "turnpikes," the term being derived from the large turnstile, made of two timbers, that the toll collector rotated on a post to allow a wagon to pass. The ends of the timbers were usually capped with a metal point and looked something like the pike, a favorite weapon of medieval infantrymen. Virginia built the first turnpike, in 1785, and Thomas Jefferson was "a moral backer of this daring venture, and many think he had a financial stake in it too."[10]

Toll roads were indeed profitable investments, and at first private companies built more roads than did local governments. Pennsylvania had the best roads and built the first major gravel road, the Philadelphia-Lancaster turnpike, in 1795. A peddler could get a wagonload of goods to Lancaster, but he still needed a pack horse to go on to Pittsburgh.

The Federal Government started a road from Cumberland, Maryland, to Wheeling, West Virginia, to connect the Potomac and Ohio rivers. It was superior to any road built since Roman times. Though it was a winding mountain road, it replaced the trails and foot-

paths with a sprawling superhighway sixty feet wide.
When it opened in 1818, it created a sensation.

With the roads came the taverns and coaching
houses, of which the peddler was a frequent visitor,
passing along his collection of news, rumors, gossip, and
lies as he made his way across the country. The popular
image of the colonial and early-American tavern is that
of a country inn made of stone, hand-hewn timbers,
wide random floorboards, with pretty barmaids and
serving wenches, pleasant fires in the nippy weather,
tankards of ale, and dinner tables loaded with pheasant
and suckling pig. There were, in fact, some splendid
taverns, but most were more primitive than charming,
and all were overrun with flies, mosquitoes, and vermin.

An English Army officer, traveling through America
in 1826, was shocked to find nine men sleeping in three
beds in an upstate New York inn.[11] Tavern owners frequently made deals with stagecoach drivers to leave
before a meal was finished, thus preventing the customers
from eating too much food, and often sparing the tavernkeeper the expense of providing a dessert the customers
had already paid for. Meals were served on a "all you
can eat" basis, and the style, if the tavernkeeper could
help it, was "gulp, gobble, and go."[12] On one occasion,
all the passengers dashed for the coach, except one
peddler, who continued to eat his meal. After he had
eaten all the roast he wanted, he called the landlord over
and asked for a spoon to eat his dessert with. When
dinner was served, the table had been set with spoons,
but now there were none in sight. The peddler told the
innkeeper that if he got the stagecoach back, he would
point out the man who took the spoons. The innkeeper,
incensed over the theft, dispatched the stable boy on a
fast horse to overtake the stage and bring it back. As it
pulled up to the tavern door, the angry innkeeper demanded that the peddler point out "the man that took
them spoons."

"Sure thing, squire," said the peddler, as he climbed into the best seat in the coach, "I'll p'int him out. I took 'em myself. You will find every one of them in the big coffeepot on the table. C'mon, driver, let's be going."[13]

As the thousands of miles of turnpikes were built, a demand for wagons created a new industry. The peddlers got wagons and loaded them until they creaked. Hugh Auchincloss (a forefather of Hugh D., stepfather of Jacqueline Kennedy Onassis) drove a mule team and wagon loaded with dry goods from New York to Louisville, peddling his way through the War of 1812, ending a "rich man," and becoming another of those "people you never heard of" who rose to wealth and affluence.

Production of goods increased rapidly, and peddler salesmanship became "the indispensable handmaid to production."[14]

As new products appeared, they were added to the tin peddler's wagon until it was a traveling store filled with baskets, books, brooms, brushes, candles, chairs, clocks, cutlery, drugs, hats, jewelry, nursery stock, patent medicines, pins, razors, shoes, silverware, spinning wheels, yarn, and woodenware, to name only part of the list.

The South did not participate in the industrial expansion or the road building. God had given them fields instead of factories, and rivers instead of roads, and they were quite content with His choices. The tobacco culture of the South created a small planter class that took a disdainful attitude toward business, and left to the Yankees the crass pursuits of commerce, with the result that until comparatively recent times, the South remained a marketplace for goods manufactured in the Northeast.

Different businesses bred different temperaments, or vice versa, and the resulting personalities were incompatible. The animosity between North and South can be seen in the antagonisms between the Yankee peddler and his southern customers. The reputation for hospitality, good breeding, and politeness struck the peddler as a

farce acted out by ruthless slaveholders, more accurately
noted, it seemed to him, for "their looseness of morals,
and their fondness for horse racing, drinking and gambling."[15]

On the other hand, the Southerner felt that the New
Englander was full of "pretended holiness and disagree-
able self-righteousness . . . [he] criticized his Yankee
shrewdness and charged him with business methods
that were little short of thievery."[16]

Others disapproved of the peddler, and they weren't
all from the South. Dr. Timothy Dwight, president of
Yale in 1823, declared that the Yankee peddlers had
parted with all modesty and principle. Young men away
from home were too free from restraining influences, and
their moral decline was certain. It is a measure of his
status that the peddler was denounced by so distinguished a critic.

Europeans found the "American spitting habit" and
the Yankee peddler appropriate symbols of our primitive
culture, according to Richardson Wright. In his account
of the wanderers of early America he cited an indignant
Englishman who claimed that "The whole race of Yankee
peddlers . . . are proverbial for dishonesty. They go
forth annually in the thousands to lie, cog, cheat, swin-
dle . . ."[17]

Another Englishman who traveled through the
States after the War of 1812 found, on the contrary, that
the "New Englanders"—peddlers, in particular—were "intelligent, sober, enterprising, and persevering. . . . When
he finds his range at home too limited . . . he finds some
nook in which he can establish himself with advantage
. . . If you see at the turnpike gate of a country town
a light carriage . . . built up all round with a pile of
assorted packing boxes and trunks—it is . . . a New
England peddler, swapping, or selling, or buying . . .
In all those byways of getting on in the world, for

which America affords unexampled facilities, none are found to succeed like the natives of New England."[18]

Whether he was hero or villain, the tin peddler was America's leading traveling salesman, and no one saw more of the country than he did, except perhaps the clock peddler.

A legend in his own time, the clock peddler was probably the first traveling salesman who had to justify the need for his product. The tin peddler's wares caught the woman's eye while he was still coming up the road. Tinware was inexpensive and useful, as were the many other things the tin peddler carried. But the clock was an expensive item, somewhat superfluous in homes when the time that mattered most was the time of year. In the selling of clocks, fact and fiction were woven into the legend of Sam Slick, Yankee clock peddler. Sam Slick was the creation of Thomas Haliburton, a Nova Scotian, and was widely enjoyed here and in London as a satire of Yankee gall and cunning. Sam Slick's favorite selling technique was to leave a clock with a family under some pretense, so they might become accustomed to it, and therefore unwilling to give it up. After complimenting the farmer on his land, his crops, his good sense, and flattering the wife with anything that came into his head, he would ask if he might not leave a clock with them for a few weeks while he did some traveling. It was his best clock, he lied, the last of its kind, and it was already sold anyway and he did not want it damaged. As Sam Slick explained, "We trust to soft sawder to get them into the house, and to human natur' that they never come out of it."

Eli Terry did, in fact, sell his clocks with this technique. On one occasion, Terry had in mind a wealthy farmer he knew who might be a likely prospect for a good clock. During a heavy rainstorm Terry rode out to the farmer's house and explained that he had been caught in the rain and feared that his clock would be damaged. He asked if he might not leave it on the farmer's mantel, where it would be safe and dry until he returned from his trip. When Terry returned, the farmer was ready to buy the clock, or more accurately, he was unwilling to part with it. The "free home trial," still popular with merchandisers today, is nothing more than a variation of this clock peddler's trick.

Terry was so successful as a clock peddler that he set up a factory which, he announced, was going to produce one thousand clocks a year. His disbelieving neighbors thought he was mad. How could he make that many clocks? And how on earth could he ever sell them? Within a few years Terry was producing and selling four thousand clocks a year, and at the time of his death in 1852, Terry left to his sons a factory with an annual production of ten to twelve thousand clocks.

Chauncey Jerome, using Terry's methods of mass production, turned out good, inexpensive clocks. He sent a boatload of them to London—the first American clocks to be exported—along with his salesman Epaphroditus Peck. British customs authorities, seeing the low prices on the clocks, suspected that the Yankee clockmaker was trying to avoid paying the full import duty. The entire shipment was seized, and Peck was given a Government check for the declared value, plus 10 percent, according to a British law designed to teach a lesson to importers who undervalued their goods. Peck, of course, was delighted. He notified Jerome and eagerly awaited another shipment. They sold the British Government three boatloads of clocks before the customs officials realized that the clocks were accurately priced.[19] Peck probably made the biggest sale in American history by keeping his mouth shut.

Clock peddlers knocked on a lot of cabin doors and did some fast talking to move that many clocks a year, and altogether they were a pretty wily group. There are many stories of the peddler selling clocks that ran just long enough for him to get his wagon out of sight. Clock peddler yarns make good reading, but they don't tell the whole story. The descendant of a Bristol clockmaker disputed the traditional view of "these early traveling salesmen." Priscilla Carrington Kline discovered a packet of letters written by clock peddlers to her great grand-father between 1831 and 1842. She particularly took exception to Wright's comment that the peddler was "a commercial bird of passage. He always left his customers convinced and satisfied with their share of the bargain, but he usually managed to clear out after finishing a deal."

Actually, as these letters make clear, the peddler often had to wait a year for his money when the crops were bad, spent idle months without income when shipments were held up, accepted payment in money of doubtless or uncertain value, and had no recourse if the customer refused to make good on his debts, since peddling was often illegal anyway, and where it wasn't, the peddler was at a disadvantage. Justice was not always uniform, being tipped slightly in favor of the resident over the transient. Some of the debts had been standing so long "that one half of the people have smartmouthed, and the balance have forgotten that they ever made such a contract . . ."

As for the money he could collect, the peddler was relieved if he could get it home before its value fluctuated wildly. Wrote one peddler, ". . . we are compelled to take Tenn Alabama and Mississippi paper and a large portion of the latter otherwise we can get nothing at all . . . There is more Shinplaster in circulation in this country than would cover the Kentucky purchase one inch thick."[20]

Sylas Holbrook, who peddled around the country in the 1820s and wrote a book about it, took an equally dim view of hinterland paper. "I have in my hand a roll that would excite envy, if not suspicion," he wrote, "that would buy little more than a dinner."[21]

The long waits for shipments, the long distance traveled between sales, bad credit, damaged goods, all added to the cost of the products sold by peddlers. As the 1800s neared the halfway mark, the railroads began to ship goods. They were putting some canals out of business almost before the digging had stopped.

While the peddler often used the canalboat as a means of transportation, the development of the canal systems tended to drive peddlers away, deeper into the interior, where goods were scarce.

The canal barge had, only a few years before, replaced the Conestoga wagon as the principal carrier of freight. Now the railroad was taking over. As the railroads extended their tracks, towns and stores grew at every crossing. There were more places to buy things, more things to buy, and at better prices and of more reliable quality than the peddler could supply. Many Yankee peddlers left the road and settled along the way to open a store. Some went back home and began to manufacture the things they had learned by experience that people wanted to buy.

By about 1840, the Yankees were leaving the business in droves. Simultaneously, the immigration of German Jews was increasing rapidly, and they found peddling a way to get their start in the new country. It has been suggested that the Jews, hard-pressed and desperate, had driven the Yankees out of the peddling business. The truth is that the Jews filled the jobs the Yankees were leaving.

The story of the Jewish peddler is a rich history of its own. Many, if not most, of the German Jews who came to the United States around 1840 took up the peddlers pack. They traveled by foot or by wagon over the back roads of the South and the West, graduating with prosperity from pack peddlers and city hawkers to merchants. A few peddlers like the Lehmans, the Selig-

mans, Adam Gimbel, and Meyer Guggenheim left legends
in their wake.

The Yankee peddler's reputation for sharp dealing
was inherited by the Jewish peddlers, and it was not
long before the Jews were blamed for every bit of Yankee
connivance.

A great deal has been written about the peddler as
American history's most unforgettable character, yet he
was not just another colorful footnote to America's past.
He was the best example of the new man created in the
New World. The Puritan and the pioneer have come to
symbolize the American experience, but the peddler was
closer to possessing all the qualities of the New American
than any of the characters of the colonial era. The peddler
was resourceful and energetic. He was a "self-starter" who
braved all the hardships and terrors that faced the
pioneers, and he did it with a pack on his back. When
conditions at home did not suit him, the young man
who chose the peddler's wandering life displayed the
American preference for mobility over quiet resignation
at home. Because of his willingness to venture out on his
own, peddlers were among the first men in the new country to rise from rags to riches, a feat then still new in
the world. An ordinary man, with no special endowments,
could accumulate wealth, possessing only the desire to
do so and the willingness to do the work and run the
risks. Skills were not necessary, nor influential friends,
or noble birth. The American Dream was born with the
peddler.

Businessmen today treat their commercial forefathers
as they would a great-grandmother who had been a
streetwalker. They might consider, however, that the
colonization of the United States was a commercial venture underwritten by stock companies for a profit, and
that commerce turned more wheels than did the quest
for religious freedom or the flight from tyranny. We were
the children of international trade and we grew up, as a

country, buying and selling, although we don't like to think of ourselves in quite this way.

From the time of the Pilgrims, selling was an art that began to acquire distinctly American characteristics. Assuming the overtones of a religion and a science, it was infused into the American man in the colonial crucible in which he was formed. He was born with the soul of a salesman—and a traveling salesman, at that.

"The American tradition," wrote Max Lerner, "has grown by movement, not by sitting." It grew from a restless people, possessed by their energy, pursuing their dreams with quickening hope. It was not natural to our tradition to sit and wait when every impulse said go and get. The peddler was in step with the mood of the times, and the territory he chose was as magnetic to him as the frontier. In fact, in most cases, it *was* the frontier.

While the number of peddlers in America did not begin to decline until 1910, the importance of the peddler to sales and distribution of goods began to decline before the Civil War. To follow the thread of our story of the traveling man, we now leave the peddler. There was a new man with new ideas on the road. He carried a trunk too, but not on a wagon. He came from back East, and when he arrived by train, the porter took his trunk for him and put him and it in a carriage bound for the best hotel in town—if there was one. The wholesale drummer had arrived.

Chapter Two

Drummer on
the Noon Train

From your own childhood you may remember a
small town, with the stores the way they used to be.
I remember my grandfather's general store in Georgia,
which, along with Mrs. Thomas' dry-goods store next door,
catered to the needs of a small farming community.

The town had been depopulating since the Civil
War. The young people moved to the cities. The old
folks died. And the sharecroppers were driven off the
land.

My grandfather, Jesse Hill, had been mayor back
when the town was incorporated, long before one thunder-
ous night when the cotton gin burned down, and having
never been rebuilt, left its twisted skeleton as a visible
symbol of decline.

The town was reddish-brown and gray, with the
exception of the green trees in summer, but even they
conformed to shades of gray in winter, and waved ocher
leaves in an unspectacular autumn.

The gasoline pump, the iron-pipe columns and tin

roof, the wooden porch common to both stores—all had corroded, rusted, and weathered into dull harmony. The highway and the tracks of the Seaboard Railroad lay between the cluster of houses and stores and the cotton fields.

The store carried a jumbled line of general goods from jawbreakers to chicken feed. Mobiles of flypaper hung in ringlets from the rafters, and a hundred odors and fragrances mixed and swirled in the currents of rising heat as the sun moved up the porch and made the loafers move their chairs and soft-drink crates.

It was quiet, until the whistle blew in the distance, and when the train screamed past it was a demon to gawk at. Only now and then did the train stop for passengers.

This is the way the town and the store were in the summer of 1940.

The first drummer probably stopped here after the Civil War and found things not much different. The gas pumps weren't there, of course, and there were more flies, and the swarm of smells inside the store was more pungent, since fewer of the groceries were in packages. The crowd on the front porch was larger, and the store was a popular gathering place for the farmers who came in to buy a few groceries or to pick up the mail and visit.

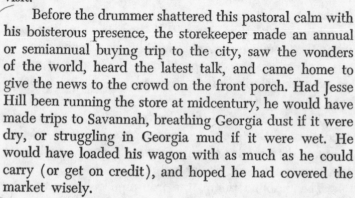

Before the drummer shattered this pastoral calm with his boisterous presence, the storekeeper made an annual or semiannual buying trip to the city, saw the wonders of the world, heard the latest talk, and came home to give the news to the crowd on the front porch. Had Jesse Hill been running the store at midcentury, he would have made trips to Savannah, breathing Georgia dust if it were dry, or struggling in Georgia mud if it were wet. He would have loaded his wagon with as much as he could carry (or get on credit), and hoped he had covered the market wisely.

When the Seaboard laid tracks through the cotton fields, the market would come to him. He would not miss the mud and the dust, but he would miss the annual touch with what was going on. The noon train from Columbus would bring a dapper stranger with a sample case, who would now be the storekeeper's informant about life in the great world beyond.

Don Marquis, recalling his own boyhood memories of the drummer, wrote: "People didn't get around much in those days. The Mississippi River was only 30 or 40 miles west of the village where I lived; but to me it was as unreal and fabulous as the Amazon or the Nile . . . And those Drummers, why they crossed it every week or so! They were in contact with the world. They traveled clean over into I'way! Anything more than 20 or 30 miles away was hard to realize."[1]

The pleasure of his trip, however, was greatly exaggerated, particularly in the first two decades of the train's existence. Horace Porter wrote an article in 1888 about travel on the first trains. The passenger, he wrote, "was jammed into a narrow seat with a stiff back, the deck of the car was low and flat, and ventilation in winter impossible. A stove at each end did little more than generate carbonic oxide. The passenger roasted if he sat at the end of the car, and froze if he sat in the middle. Tallow candles furnished a 'dim religious light,' but the accompanying odor did not savor of cathedral incense. The dust was suffocating in dry weather; there were no adequate spark arresters on the engine, or screens at the windows, and the begrimed passenger at the end of his journey looked as if he had spent the day in a blacksmith shop."

The fear of sudden death hung in the air like the coal smoke. Danger lurked even in the rails, which were "cut diagonally, so that when laid down they would lap and form a smoother joint. Occasionally they became sprung; the spikes would not hold, and the end of the

rail with its sharp point rose high enough for the wheel
to run under it, rip it loose, and send the pointed end
through the floor of the car. This was called a "snake's
head," and the unlucky being sitting over it was likely to
be impaled against the roof . . . spitted like a Christmas
turkey."[2]

The first drummers must have created quite a stir
in Jesse Hill's store, all dressed up "like one of them
magazine pitchers." He would have been the most note-
worthy event in that somnolent wayside since the cotton-
gin fire. Theodore Dreiser has a description of one in
Sister Carrie:

"Here was a type of the traveling canvasser for a
manufacturing house—a class which at that time was first
being dubbed by the slang of the day 'drummers.' He
came within the meaning of a still newer term, which
had sprung into general use among Americans in 1880,
and which concisely expressed the thought of one whose
dress or manners are calculated to elicit the admiration
of susceptible young women—'a masher.' His suit was of
a striped and crossed pattern of brown wool, new at
that time, but since become familiar as a business suit.
The low crotch of the vest revealed a stiff shirt bosom
of white and pink stripes. From his coat sleeves protruded
a pair of linen cuffs of the same pattern, fastened with
large, gold-plate buttons, set with the common yellow
agates known as 'cat's eyes.' His fingers bore several rings
. . . and from his vest dangled a neat gold watch chain,
from which was suspended the secret insignia of the
Order of Elks. The whole suit was rather tight-fitting,
and was finished off with heavy-soled tan shoes, highly
polished, and the gray fedora hat." Somewhat to his
credit, the drummer was "actuated not by greed, but
an insatiable love of variable pleasure."[3]

The drummer was already known to the country
merchants who did their annual buying in the big wholesale districts back East. In New York, he was known as

the Pearl Street drummer. Asa Green, a New Englander
who went to New York in 1830 and became editor of
the New York *Evening Transcript,* wrote that ". . . the
practice of drumming is held by some to be neither
modest nor very dignified, still it must be owned to add
pretty largely, in certain cases, to the account of goods
sold . . . [although drumming] is not very highly esteemed in Pearl Street."[4]

Dressed in a flamboyant version of the latest fashion,
he was the resident not of Pearl Street, where the wholesale houses were, but of the hotel lobbies, where the
country merchants checked into the Astor House and
other first-class hotels of the day.

The country man, dressed in his Sunday go-to-meetin'
clothes, was not hard to spot, and a quick glance at
the hotel registry or a word with the bellhop would resolve any doubts.

He would immediately be set upon by the suave
drummer, who offered him dinner, theater tickets, or a
look at the after-dark sights. The drummer was ready to
lead him to his pleasure. Gerald Carson has written that
the drummer was as ready to take the merchant "to a
church as to an assignation and praise him loudly, too,
for his preference."[5] One drummer said that when he
called on a storekeeper he always carried a Bible and a
flask.

The wholesale drummer was not the invention of
Pearl Street. In the thriving trade along the Persian Gulf
around 2000 B.C., merchants had sent out their goods
with independent commercial travelers. The ancient
Greeks had used wholesale dealers—*emporos*—who sold
by samples, which they displayed either in the market or
carried about from place to place.

The English wholesalers employed "hookers-in" and
"canvassing clerks," who scoured the taverns and coaching houses for the arrival of buyers, and "riders out,"
who met the buyers halfway to London. In the eighteenth

century the "rider out" carried samples and solicited
business for wholesale cloth merchants among the drapers
in the country.

To Washington Irving, in 1819, English commercial
travelers appeared as successors of the knights-errant,
who, "instead of vindicating the charms of peerless
beauty . . . rode about, spreading the fame and standing
of some substantial tradesman or manufacturer, and are
ready at any time to bargain in his name, it being the
fashion nowadays to trade instead of fight . . ."[6]

A writer in 1839 described the English commercial
traveler as a "generally young and very shrewd individual,
possessing great suavity of manner, and a remarkable
ability to suit himself to all the varied moods of his
very various customers."[7] In France and Germany, the
traveling salesman was already well-established in a growing and respectable profession.

Many of the first traveling salesmen in America were
former English travelers, and their loud dress and brassy
manners, Gerald Carson estimates, did much to nurture
the rural American distaste for both Englishmen and salesmen.

We are indebted to Mr. Carson for rescuing from
historical oblivion the existence of Merit Welton, a button
salesman for the Scovil Manufacturing Company of
Waterbury, Connecticut, who made a trip through the
Midwest in 1832 to sell buttons by sample. He did not
accept chickens, cottonseed, or wood ashes in payment,
nor did he sell any buttons on the spot. He took orders,
demanded payment in cash, and deliveries were made
later by freight. Mr. Welton was the first drummer, so
far as we know, and his trip was not a success. (The
first three letters in Scovil, by the way, were later to
become the last three letters in Ansco, formed by way
of merger.)

The new traveling man did not appear in great
numbers until wholesale houses sent drummers out to

check on accounts after the panic of 1837. They carried
samples and took orders where credit was good. The
Society of Commercial Travelers said the term "drummer"
came into vogue around 1854, when the "business of
those who travelled for commercial firms was confined to
soliciting a continuance of previous orders, and making
collections and new acquaintances, within an extremely
narrow limit of trade . . ."[8]

Many wholesale merchants objected to the practice
of sending out drummers, on the grounds that it ruined
the business. One old-timer complained that when he was
a hardware jobber there was some dignity to it. "We
didn't send a man out to every crossroads hamlet looking
for orders, but we stayed at home and the dealers came
to us. Every customer had his order book in a separate
pigeon hole on the wall of the sample room, and he
was proud of the fact and glad to have an account with
us . . .

"Now its all a scramble for orders and devil take
the hindmost."[9] There were, he felt, only so many goods
to be sold and so many places to sell them, and they
would all be sold without all this unseemly running
around. He darkly concluded that the man who first put
a salesman on the road did a bad thing.

In spite of such skepticism, many selling practices
originated with men who traveled and experienced first-
hand the vagaries of the marketplace. Trade and Mark
Smith (William and Andrew) traveled the Hudson
River and the Catskills, selling large jars of cough drops
to the country merchants. In 1866, after they had inherited the business from their father, they were bothered
with imitators who offered cough drops under the name
of Schmidt Brothers, Smith and Brothers, or some such
plagiarism. To identify their product, the Smith Brothers
used a trademark—one of the first, and still famous. (Bull
Durham chewing tobacco had appeared a year earlier.)
They also began to use "factory-filled packages." While

they were not the first to package a product, they were the first to successfully capitalize on the practice. "Production of cough drops . . . jumped from five pounds to five tons."[10]

The use of factory-filled packages became almost mandatory, and a little slogan on the package carried by the soda-cracker drummer reads today like social comment:

> For in my package sealed and tight,
> My maker keeps me pure and white.[11]

Perley G. Gerrish is credited as the discoverer of market testing. He was a drummer for Squirrel Brand assorted nuts and had made, on his own, a peanut bar which none of his customers would buy. Gerrish loaded a wagon and drove from Boston to Providence, handing out free samples to school children. When he covered his territory next time, he found merchants, softened by the children's crusade, eager to stock peanut bars.

In 1911, another drummer, Charles Coolidge Parlin, compiled the first comprehensive market-research study, although market research did not become popular until the late 1940s, after the buying spree that greeted the end of the war subsided.

In the first years when salesmen called on them, merchants and storekeepers were glad to be able to look at samples and order goods without having to leave the store. But before many years passed, the buyer was overrun with salesmen who grew more persistent as the competition increased.

While the wholesaler may have felt a loss of dignity in going after business—how much more magnificent to sit back and let it come to you—it was the drummer who bore the brunt of the buyer's ingratitude for the sudden attention that the commercial world had thrust upon him. It was not unheard of for a drummer to be thrown out, left waiting for long hours, or told to come back tomorrow

by a storekeeper who had no intention of buying anything, a disaster for a man who had to keep moving to
make a living.

Some buyers were sympathetic with the drummer and his problems. One wrote, "There is for the ordinary drummer a weary monotony in it that becomes very wearing—the constant jumping from
one point to another, with the long inactive rides;
the sameness of hotel existence; the waiting about
to get a chance to talk to the man he must see; the
sense of being alone for weeks at a time, without
meeting a person with whom he can share his inner
personal life, or who has more than a passing interest in his success or failure; the pressure of his
house behind him urging him to more strenuous endeavor, and his competitors making things as hot for
him as they conveniently can."[12]

Being rude to drummers was part of running a store,
but despite his easy smiles and grand gestures, the
drummer was not always willing to accept abuse as part
of his job. Charles S. Plummer recalled a drummer who,
incensed at the storekeeper's insolence, reached over the
counter and decked him with one clip. The surprised
storekeeper sat sputtering and blinking on the floor while
the drummer gave him a brief lecture on the rudiments
of courtesy. They talked it over and had a glass of
wine, both apologizing, and the drummer wrote up a
small order.[13]

Drummers were liable for arrest in many states, and
they began to form their own organizations to improve
the sort of welcome that they were getting from city
detectives and sheriffs. The old ordinances that plagued
the peddlers and drove many out of the field were now
used against the drummers, and new ones were written
to outlaw selling by sample.

At the time the Society of Commercial Travelers

was meeting in New York in 1869, Henry Dreshler of Newark had languished in the Baltimore jail for five weeks, awaiting trial for "selling goods without a license." The Maryland law called for a fine of $400 to $600 for each offense. The cost of a license was $300, good for one year, and in 1869 that was a prohibitive figure.

In the 1880s the Texas Legislature passed a law requiring "drummers, fortune tellers, cock fighters and clairvoyants"[14] to buy a license for $200. In addition to this, the tax receipt had to be recorded in the county seat of each county visited. The traveling men caused as much inconvenience as they could to those charged with enforcing the laws. Howard Peak, an early Texas drummer, saw a man following him out of town making great haste. Peak was driving a wagon, and he poured it on his team. The man, after eating several miles of wagon dust, finally caught up with him and, as he had guessed, it was the sheriff, who wanted to see Peak's license. Peak calmly handed it to him, properly recorded.

A good practical joke in the trade was simply to walk up behind a commercial traveler, tap him on the shoulder and watch him pale, or to pound on the door of another salesman's room, knowing full well he had his samples set up for display.

The stiffest laws against the first drummers in the mid-1800s came from cities that sent out thousands of drummers themselves. From Baltimore, Philadelphia, and Pittsburgh, ten thousand traveling salesmen sold the products of growing factories and mills. Another ten thousand travelers went out from Cincinnati, Chicago, and St. Louis, twenty thousand from New York, and ten thousand from Boston and the New England states. Each city wanted to sell the nation and yet shut out other drummers from selling to them.

The Society of Commercial Travelers viewed this with a fine rage. "Abolish the commercial traveler," they warned, "shut him out from your states, drive him from your cities, and you return to provincialism, inferiority, absence of variety, uncertain supply, monopoly, and high prices."[15] And that wasn't all. They said the hotels and railroads would suffer and business everywhere would grow sluggish. But they needn't have worried. No one was going to foil the growing legions of irrepressible drummers.

The Society said there were 50,000 travelers in 1869. A few years later, the New York *Herald* said there must be at least 100,000 drummers, and maybe as many as 500,000. Other estimates ran as high as 800,000 by 1910. Census figures were lower, and apparently somewhat misleading. One indication I have that the Government figures were low is that in 1908, the seven largest insurance companies selling accident insurance exclusively to commercial travelers had over 247,000 subscribers, and yet the 1900 census claimed only 93,000 traveling salesmen.

Raymond Ries compiled a chart listing the number of workers in the various sales categories, and according to it there were, in addition to the 93,000 commercial travelers, 76,649 "hucksters and peddlers" and 241,162 "sales agents." In 1900, then, 410,730 people were selling in some ambulatory fashion. How many drummers were there? It depended on how you defined the term.

All the figures agreed on one thing: There were more traveling men every year. The drummer laws were eventually declared unconstitutional, and the Society of Commercial Travelers and other traveling men's associations moved on to other battles, feeling for the first time some collective power.

They would need power, for it was the railroad that concerned them most. The drummer's samples were his life. The railroad took a cavalier attitude about their transportation, declaring that baggage "shall consist of wearing apparel, toilet articles, and similar effects." As far as the railroad was concerned, a two hundred-pound iron-bound trunk of samples did not constitute "baggage"; therefore, they took no responsibility for it. If it arrived, it was baggage. If it got lost, it was samples.

Even this was better than the system, or lack of a system, with which the first train-borne salesmen contended. "Baggage checks and coupon tickets were unknown. Long trips had to be made over lines composed of a number of short, independent railways; and at the terminus of each the bedeviled passenger had to transfer, purchase another ticket, personally pick out his baggage, perhaps on an uncovered platform in a rainstorm, and take his chances of securing a seat . . ."[16]

The modern traveling man of the late 1800s wanted the railroads to pay for the lost samples and for loss of time, citing the experience of one salesman whose samples had been lost during the peak of the Christmas ordering season. A "baggage smasher fired a squirt of tobacco juice at the check," and the vital trunk wound up in Mississippi instead of the "Mass" town for which it was intended.[17]

Some of the other grievances aired in the meeting halls of the traveling man's club may have seemed trivial. Fire exits in all hotels, and better freight and passenger rates were of obvious importance, but abolishing the roller towel and requiring that all hotels and boardinghouses provide nine-foot sheets were not likely to become popular rallying cries. Only a traveling salesman could fully appreciate the sight of a damp, soiled roller towel after extensive public use. A salesman who complained about an overripe roller towel was informed by the landlord that men had been using that towel all week, and he was the first one to complain.

The nine-foot sheet was the first defense against bedbugs and vermin that inhabited hotel beds in pre-pesticide days, being long enough to tuck in at the foot and still leave enough sheet to fold over the blankets.

E. M. Statler, the moving genius behind the modern

hotel, got most of his ideas on hotel innovations by chatting with drummers in the smoking car. His hotels were designed to please these critical travelers. In the days before Statler built his first big hotel in Buffalo, in 1907, most hotels offered one bathroom to a floor. Heat and hot water were unreliable, and "no proprietor called his house really full until all the double beds were fully occupied, often by bedmates who were complete strangers."[18] Statler's hotels all had private baths, something not even the Waldorf could boast. He provided sample rooms for traveling salesmen, free newspaper delivery, fast laundry and dry-cleaning service—for which the traveling salesman was, and still is, the best customer. (Sometimes a traveling salesman, arriving late at night, would hang his suit in the shower, turn on the hot water, and let the steam take out the wrinkles. Frequently he would forget about it, and wet plaster and hot water would shower the hapless tenants of the room below.)

Statler once said that "A shoe salesman and a traveling prince want essentially the same things when they are on the road—namely good food and a comfortable bed—and that is what I propose to give them."[19] Because of Statler's influence, the traveling public got all the hotel reforms they sought without further effort. Going beyond a concern for their personal comfort and safety, the commercial travelers of the late 1800s began to express themselves on larger issues. The Sound Money Commercial Travelers declared that they would be a permanent guard to the nation's credit, and they spoke importantly, to little effect, against the evils of silver coinage, which would debase the currency. A hundred-man delegation of travelers called on President McKinley to discuss the matter, and he received them warmly. "There was a popular belief," wrote Don Marquis, "that the Drummer of America was a mighty force which no candidate could buck against. We believed . . . the Drummers had had a lot to do with turning the country for

McKinley and the Gold Standard. The Drummers had
got their orders from Big Business, the story was—possibly
from Mark Hanna himself—and they had gone all over
the country telling the small businessman that financial
and industrial ruin would ensue unless Bryan were de-
feated."[20]

The Travelers Protective Association of America was
reorganized from a fraternal smoker to a company that
provided accident coverage and death "benefits." When
seven thousand members converged on Milwaukee in
1892, old man Pabst stood in the driveway of his brewery
and handed out beer to the men as they drove past.

At one convention, a distillery placed a fresh jug of
whiskey at each salesman's door every morning.

The annual meetings were tumultuous affairs concerned with what to fight for next, but when it came to
electing officers and selecting the sight for the next convention, the meetings lasted through the night and past
breakfast, teetering on the brink of general fist fighting.

The Commercial Travelers Club of New York, in contrast, was associated with the Sound Money crowd and
above such partisan bickering. They had clambakes with
the Union League Club and held quiet weekly smokers
for entertainment and serious discussion. The Club provided an impressive setting where members of a respectable profession met out-of-town customers, played bil-
liards, relaxed, swapped stories amid potted palms in
dark-paneled rooms lined with deep orientals, overstuffed
chairs, and highly polished brass. There was an air of
assurance about the place.

In upstate New York, the cornerstone was laid for a
posh retirement home for drummers and their families.
Men like Chauncey Depew, then president of the New
York Central, were raising money for it, and fund-raising
exhibitions were held in the then fashionable Madison
Square Garden.

The drummer was enjoying a kind of golden age.

Book salesmen looked back on the era as the "silk hat days of book travelers . . . [when] a representative of a great publishing house was a business representative of importance who should travel well, live well and be treated well."[21]

Commercial men in an expansive commercial age, they were everybody's darlings. Well, not everybody's. To the farmer, they were the agents of the urban conspiracy, reviving the ancient antagonism between the farmer and the city man, and recalling the legend that Damascus, the oldest city in the world, was built upon the spot where Cain slew Abel, thus giving all cities, through the ages, the "brand of Cain."[22]

The country man saw the land as the principal source of wealth and virtue, and the city traders and middlemen as bandits who cheated him out of a fair price for his farm goods and inflated the price of "store boughten" goods with their everlasting unearned commissions.

The farmer was caught by his increasing dependence on manufactured goods and the declining status of agriculture in the national life. The drummer was just another nonproducing commission parasite as far as the farmer was concerned, but his citified ways repelled and attracted. In spite of the fact that his loathing ran deep and was held with classic peasant tenacity, the farmer was made the gullible victim of every dishonest drummer and agent who cared to make the effort.

There was a vast difference between the traveling man with a territory and the fly-by-night agent out for what he could get, with no plans to return. It stands to reason that the traveling man trying to build up a steady clientele along his regular route was bound to more honorable intentions than if he kept going without looking back. The wholesale drummer making regular calls on dealers was a pretty straight arrow. The agent, who was really a fancy peddler, was often a rogue. It was he who victimized the farmer and his small-town neighbors.

The patent-right agents, medicine hawkers, book agents, lightning-rod salesmen, land speculators, tombstone swindlers, and tree peddlers were part of that "class of Eastern producers and vendors who had been brought up in a much more sophisticated type of urbanism . . ."[23]

The traveling tree salesman was particularly successful in the prairies of the West. Most of the settlers there were from back East and unaccustomed to the treeless plains. They longed for fruit trees and woodlands, and the tree agent promised to make the desert bloom. A farm magazine in 1883 described the two types of tree salesmen as a "horny-handed man with duck overalls . . . and a kid-glove tree peddler." The latter wore "a plug hat, high-heeled boots and [was] 'all shined up,' with a carpetbag full of fine fruit plates, and large whole fruit made of wax . . . This tree peddler is your horticultural dude. He goes abroad seeking whom he may devour . . . His trees are borer proof. They are of the Russian variety," meaning they were supposed to survive in impossibly low temperatures. "Your dude tree peddler is a man of gab. His tongue is as long as your arm, as oily as a piece of bacon, and loose as a calf's tail in fly-time. He pays his attention to your wife and shows his wax fruit to your daughters. He knows he will sell second-class trees that he will get from a neighboring nursery when it comes time to make his delivery."[24]

It was hard to tell straight arrow from dude, for they were both likely to be wonderfully dressed and uncommonly wordy, if not articulate.

George Ade wrote a play, produced in 1903, that reflected some of the sentiment of those early days. Miss Lorena Watkins, the village milliner, is talking to Whittaker, the drummer for the S. W. Perkins Duplex Wind Pump Co.:

"Oh, its been the ambition of my life to see Chicago," she gasps.

He replies: "It's the grandest city in the world. We're crawling up on St. Louis every day."

She says: "It must be superb. Just think of it, buildings six stories high! I've had so many traveling gentlemen tell me about it. Do you know, I love drummers! They're so much more refined than most of the men around here."[25]

The village maid and farmer's daughter were not the only ones impressed by the early drummers. Many a sleepy store clerk came suddenly to life and saw visions of his future when the traveling man visited the store.

Walter Moody, Herbert Casson, John Fresh, Frank Will Smith, and E. P. Briggs were all traveling salesmen during the 1800s, and all wrote books about their experiences. Walter Moody told of his own experience in answering the call. Bored with the routine of dusting and putting up stock, he was suddenly transfixed when a drummer sailed in on a flood of rhetoric. The young clerk hid behind a pile of damask and listened to the conversation between the salesman and the store manager. "In the selling talk of that dapper salesman lurked the gems of a new life for me. I was inoculated with a burning desire . . . the determination to become a salesman seized me on the spot . . . I was at the foot of the mountain . . ."[26]

Herbert Casson wrote about his first memories of the drummer, and for many a farm boy his experience was typical. "When I was a lad in a retail shop in the early '80s in a remote village in Canada, the coming of a traveling salesman was a great event. He remained in the village a day, and that day was one of the few shining days of the year.

"Always, he entertained us. He told us the stories and gossip of the big world, which we had never seen. He was full of fun, wisdom, news, ideas, personal talk. In the evening we all gathered in a little hotel and listened to him until ten o'clock, when all good villagers went to bed."[27]

In a fictionalized account of his own life, Earl Lamar Denham wrote that as a boy it was his original intention to become President of the United States until he saw his first drummer. "He wore a derby, spats, fancy vest, striped trousers, nose glasses, patent leather shoes, and carried a cane which he kept twirling around his finger . . . He was perfectly at ease—though country folk during those times were resentful at what they termed 'city slickers,' and within fifteen minutes from the time he arrived he had the whole crowd laughing at his jokes. Thirty minutes longer made him friends who would have punched your nose had you dared criticize him."[28]

In 1884, John Fresh wrote about his youthful dreams to be off on the road armed with stuff to sell. As a farm boy he stole a visiting drummer's samples of hoop skirts and tried to sell one to the farmer's wife nearby but was apprehended and soundly thrashed. "Time rolled on, and I was kept at school for the next four or five years, but the fixed idea of becoming a drummer never left my mind, and so impressed was I with it, that it used to haunt my very dreams, and many a picture I drew of the 'glorious life I would lead when I finally cut the apron strings' and became a drummer in fact."[29]

Frank Will Smith worked in a drugstore in Columbus, Ohio, in 1880. He swept, polished, mopped, dusted, and dreamed of becoming either an actor or a drummer. The drummers all wore "plug hats" and conjured up a "glamourous mental picture," and that swayed him.[30]

All over America, the farmers' sons, clerks, stockroom boys, and messengers stood lost in their daydreams and gaped at the snappy drummer who breezed in and out as he passed through the country. They memorized his jokes and his selling talk, and as nearly as possible they imitated his gestures and his postures.

Just as peddling had offered young men of colonial

New England a chance to get ahead, commercial traveling caught the fancy of the youth of the nation. The
success ethic became firmly associated with selling, and
in some instances remains so even today.

And just as peddlers were suspected of lowering
their moral standards when they were away from home,
so too were drummers thought to wink at the Ten Com-
mandments while they galavanted around the countryside.

The traveling man soon had a reputation as a big
spender, a drinker, a storyteller, and a flashy dresser, but
many were like E. P. Briggs. A good, hard-working drummer and a sober and humorless man, he started traveling when he and the business were young, and stayed
with it fifty years.

A drummer's grip in one hand and a sample case in
the other, a short bewhiskered man with sad, proud eyes,
he survives in a photograph, taken on the steps of a commercial hotel. A foulard tie, vest, and watch fob were
the common accouterments of dress to gentlemen of the
time, but shapeless pants with bulges at the knees gave
Briggs away as one who spent a lot of time sitting on
trains and traveling too much to keep the sharp crease
in his trousers that drummers were so fond of.

Edward P. Briggs, born in 1839 in upstate New York,
began to sell goods as a traveling salesman on September
5, 1861. He traveled in hardware, one of the first men in
that line, the practice having been started only six years
earlier, in 1855, by a man named Simmons. He was photo-
graphed on the hotel steps in 1911 with a sample case
and a valise that pulled on his arms for a half century and
made his shoulders thick and his arms longer than they
should have been.

He did his traveling with a great iron-bound trunk,
and he and it spent many hours on station platforms, in
all kinds of weather, at all times of the day and night,
waiting on trains that might be hours late.

He left the road once, toward the middle of his life, to become a partner in the firm. It went bankrupt. He said he had looked forward to getting to know his family, but he went back on the road with a new company, and the last record of him is a letter written in 1912 from a hotel in Oklahoma: fifty years on the road and still going, talking about manhood and self-discovery.[31]

Other men got more enjoyment out of their life on the road and had more success out of it, although I hesitate to say which was the cause and which was the effect. Frank Will Smith, the young drugstore clerk who wanted so badly to become a drummer, got his chance one morning when his boss decided to go into the wholesale drug business and gave him a chance to try his hand at drumming. He spent one week a month calling on the trade in a horse and buggy. One day he got the "cream territory" when the best salesman was out. He set out for a two-week trip through the Ohio coal fields, and down the Ohio River to the West Virginia line, and he sat nervously in the smoker of the Hocking Valley Railroad on what he called "that eventful morning."

Smith had his share of the adventures he craved as a round-eyed clerk. Before this trip was over, the Ohio River went on its spring rampage, and the porter banged on the door and told him he had better hustle because the river was in. He waded out of the hotel and up the gangplank of a steamboat fortunately located out front, bound for Gallipolis.

From the late 1830s to the turn of the century, the steamboat was a preferred way to travel. Passenger trains gradually took over, but it was not until George Pullman introduced the sleeping car and the parlor car in the 1860s that the train could rival the steamboat in comfort. The single greatest drawback to the steamboat was the risk of boiler explosion, often caused when the captain tied down the safety valve to make better time. There

were steamboat explosions in which more than 200 people died.

Smith, fortunately, was marooned on a more leisurely
vessel, and for eight days he played pool by day and ten-
cent poker by night, regaled by a liquor salesman from
Kentucky who set 'em up for all the boys, while houses
and chicken coops floated south down the Ohio.

The coal strikes were going on at that time, and one
lasted for seven months. The miners were incensed over
a series of articles in the Ohio *State Journal,* and every
stranger was suspected of being the reporter who had
written them. Smith was fired at a couple of times and subsequently attached a streamer to his buggy displaying
the company name. As he drove into New Straitsville one
evening, he and his companions found the population in
a state of revengeful excitement. The town marshal, who
was popular with the miners and with the townspeople,
had been shot and killed. Smith could not sleep that
night and went out early in the morning for a walk before breakfast. From a lone tree on Main Street dangled
the body of the man who, in the mob's opinion, had shot
the marshal.

On a later trip, near Coshocton, Ohio, a man jumped
out from a cluster of jack pines and grabbed for Smith's
horse. Smith whacked the horse and left the man
sprawled in the road. The next morning Smith drew open
his window curtain, and there was the man who had
attacked him, hanging from a tree. He had been arrested
for rape and taken out of jail and hung before the sun
came up.

In his ripe old age, Smith boasted that he had never
made a single claim on his accident insurance after
spending a lifetime on the road. One of the younger salesmen said, "Pop, they're saving you for a hanging."

John Fresh, the young lad who stole the drummer's
hoops, began his career with a bit of precocious peddling

that caught the attention of a wholesale dealer, who offered him a regular job as a traveler.

At fifteen, Fresh had mixed up a glue recipe and set off to peddle it. The first day, he cleared $30 and returned home in gloating triumph. After a two-week trip, he returned home with $566 in cash plus a variety of trinkets taken in trade.

He took a partner who had a horse and wagon, and to demonstrate their product they glued the harness together—traces, reins, and halter. For four days they did well, but on the fifth day it began to rain. The glue, they soon discovered, was water soluble. The wagon crashed into a tree, demolishing it and their entire stock.

Fresh later became a regular drummer with a successful route filled with good customers and amicable young ladies.

After twenty years, he was made a partner and general manager of his firm, the ascension dreamed of by every drummer who wore spats and carried a satchel.

Drummers like Briggs, Fresh, and Smith called on regular customers year after year. Mutual trust and respect replaced the usual hostile confrontation between buyer and seller. It was with great pride that men like these looked back over their life on the road, spent traveling about the country, successful in their calling, esteemed by society. Arch Trawick, a Nashville grocery drummer, recalled a trip he made in his two-horse buggy during the 1890s. "It was February and cold, about ten degrees," he wrote in a letter to his family. "There was a skim of snow; but the two horses jogged along . . . and landed me in Gallatin about five o'clock. I couldn't move. I had forgotten that it was cold. Had a good lap robe and all but there I was stuck hard and fast." The hotel proprietor helped him out of the buggy and gave him a good shot of whiskey and the kind of treatment that was due a king of the road. "At supper, I found myself sitting down to a banquet of deliciously cooked birds and all the trimmings . . . Folks in the main dining room probably looked at our feast and wondered, how come!"[32]

A Vermont marble salesman, whose name I do not know, must have bragged to all his family and friends about an unusual sale he made on Sunday morning in a North Carolina drugstore. Sitting at the soda fountain, he struck up a conversation with what he thought was a village rustic, who inquired about what business brought this Yankee to town. The drummer replied that he was traveling in monuments and tombstones, and when the old codger asked if he had Confederate monuments, he must have looked around for someone to enjoy the joke with. The salesman solemnly took out his book and showed the man pictures of Confederate monuments. The old fellow asked how much was that there one, and the drummer told him $15,000. "Ship me one," he said.

The salesman went over to the druggist for a pen and quietly inquired if the old man was crazy. The druggist assured him that if Mr. Robert Henry Ricks had ordered it, he had better ship it. The flabbergasted drummer shipped it, and it stands today at the entrance of Battle Park in Rocky Mount. Mr. Ricks, it turned out, was indeed quite wealthy, and he was also a veteran of the Civil War. The Daughters of the Confederacy had been wrangling for years over where to put a monument, although they had raised only $7000 toward its purchase. Mr. Ricks settled the matter.*

When the drummers whose feet and spirit had begun to move in the nineteenth century left the road to retire or to die, it was clear that the world they knew was changing. One of the last was George Darr, who was a telegrapher in Mount Gilead, Ohio, in 1871. He went on the road as a drummer because of "nervous trouble," and he always began his trips on the early 6:10 train to

* Mrs. Branson Hobbs told me this story. Her father knew Mr. Ricks.

Toledo. His son recorded in his diary, many years later, that his earliest memories of his father were of his leaving home for one of his trips. "I would hear Dad and Mother downstairs, and smell the bacon and eggs, but I would be too sleepy to get up. Finally the stairway door would open and I would hear Dad coming up the stairs. He would lean over the bed, and I would feel his freshly shaven cheek against mine as he kissed me good-by. Then a few minutes later I would hear the two blasts of the engine's whistle as the 6:10 pulled out of the station bound for Toledo with Dad aboard. Then I would go back to sleep." Many years later, the son was called home as the father was dying. When the old man saw his son, he said, "John, may I die?"

"And I, summoning all the self-control I had, took his hand and replied, 'Yes, Dad.' . . . Finally, with a kind of sigh, he slipped away. And at that moment the 6:10 train pulled out of the station with two blasts of the whistle . . ."[33]

The end of the golden age was at hand. By 1910, the status of the traveling man had sagged badly. Some businessmen spoke nostalgically of the "old-time drummer" who told jokes, jollied the buyer, and engaged in what had come to be known as personality selling, and the passing of the drummer was noted, by some, with indignity. "Why should this type be abolished? Why should we now have bloodless clerks as travelers, thrusting their unwelcome cards and samples into the faces of retainers and dashing for the next train?"[34]

Even as early as 1900, a few sour notes were heard: ". . . the salesmen of the newer generation exhibit more of a dead level of mediocrity. . . . There is a tendency in these days of special hurry and everlasting bustle to reduce everything to routine, and it may be that the newer men . . . show more of machine and less of individuality than the veterans . . .

"There is a greater percentage of salesmen stopping

at the second-class hotels, underdressed in appearance
and smoking cheap cigars . . ."[35]

Don Marquis, in his reminiscences of the drummer,
wrote: "The old sailing-ship reached its highest point
of usefulness and beauty just before it was superseded by
steam. And the old-fashioned Drummer bumped the ze-
nith of his era in the last years before the Salesman
came." The Salesman was "a standardized product of
modern efficiency, and he sells billions of dollars' worth
of other standardized products without telling a single
funny story or attending a lodge meeting."[36]

In the 1920s, while his numbers grew steadily, "the
salesman [was] ridiculed . . . as a miserable flunky em-
bodying the worst characteristics . . . of the commercial
world . . ."[37]

The clubs and organizations of the first drummers
disbanded or survived as accident-insurance companies,
one of which now proudly advertises that no salesman
will call. The magnificent retirement home proposed in
Binghamton never got beyond the laying of the cornerstone.

Thousands of men who were busily at work as traveling salesmen perceived the change with bitterness. Some
never noticed at all.

John Henry Patterson, of whom we will hear more
later, was to use his cold and eccentric genius to make the
drummers get in line. He made them more effective salesmen, and they earned more money, but his discovery that
a salesman could be trained and his efforts measured
took a lot of fun out of the business.

Chapter Three

Daddy Was a Traveling Man

The most durable legacy of the drummers of the last half of the nineteenth century was a collection of yarns, anecdotes, and tall tales that are known today as traveling-salesman jokes. Few of the actual jokes are still making the rounds. The traveling-salesman joke is in the oblivion of the attic of lost Americana, stored with Pat and Mike, the knock-knocks, and the little moron. The term, however, has assumed a generic function to describe a school of humor revolving around the aggressive sexual ideals of those men who are amused to imagine themselves as modern Don Juans.

There was a kind of brutal maleness involved in the mystique of the drummer that also drew on the image of the conquering invader who sold a bill of goods and slept with the farmer's daughter. The humor by and about the first drummers reveals a good deal of aggressiveness on their part and mixtures of admiration and hostility in the feelings toward them on the part of the general public. The drummer was a daring, sophisticated adventurer, but he was never on secure grounds of total respectability. Like actors, circus artists, and croupiers, he was often admired for the way he performed, but he carried a faint odor in society, expressed by a New York *grand dame* in her shock at discovering that she was seated next to a traveling salesman at a dinner in Cincinnati. "At home," she said, "commercials don't mix with the best people."

"Yes," he said, "and apparently they don't here either." An admirable retort and in keeping with the ideal of all traveling men since the peddlers—that a ready wit is more valuable than social position.

In such anecdotes as this, and in the great volume of jokes and doggerel about drummers between 1850 and the turn of the century, we find ample evidence of their peculiarly ambivalent status. The popularity of jokes about drummers clearly indicated the public's interest, but the nature of the jokes—indeed, the fact that there were jokes—also reflected an easy familiarity, condescension, and outright hostility.

The old drummers invented jokes and lived anecdotes. They listened to jokes, remembered them, carried them with them to tell their customers and the boys in the smoker. If a drummer was considered a seasoned professional, it was said of him that "he knew all the jokes."

Most of the jokes were about the realities of life on the road: cantankerous buyers, bedbugs, bad food, seedy hotels, unfaithful wives, and, of course, the farmer's daughter. The life of the drummer is more graphically described in the jokes about it than in any of the many autobiographies of traveling salesmen written during this era.

The drummer had burst upon the quiet towns and cities across America with only slightly less impact than the spewing locomotives that bore him. After the Civil

War, the country was changing fast as new inventions
came at dazzling speed—the typewriter, refrigerated
freight, the telephone, the phonograph, the automobile,
electric power, and at the turn of the century, the airplane. To many Americans who lived in small towns and
villages, the drummer was about as well-traveled as anyone they knew, and he was therefore a representative of
the new world a-building. He was a city man, and the
cities were the first beneficiaries of the new technology.
He could speak with easy familiarity of things about
which they had only heard.

The drummer, between the Civil War and the turn
of the century, rode the crest of the waves of change. He
went places when most people stayed home and dreamed
about it. His energetic and persistent efforts to sell more
goods were firmly sanctified by the Protestant ethic and
certified to be in the true tradition of Horatio Alger,
but they were made more manly and respectable by a
tolerance for hard liquor and an eye for the girls.

With the coming of the railroad, other men
wandered down to the depot to watch the big locomotives, to see the trains that steamed across America, and
they saw a drummer step off and look around—a stranger
who acted as if he owned the place, who was at home
with the wonders of the age. He cut a splendid figure,
and thought so himself.

Other men reached into their own pockets for the
money to buy their needs and few pleasures, but the
drummer was the first heir to that corporate largess, the
expense account. He had money to spend, and when he
was on the road he had his freedom. He was away from
the all-probing eyes of the neighbors and the wagging
tongues of gossips. He could drink, smoke black cigars,
play poker, swap stories, flirt with the waitress, and over-
tip the bellhop without being admonished by his wife.

He had the comforts of home and family and the
cover of anonymity to conceal his sins while he was on

the road. To those other men who felt restrained by too much Victorian togetherness, the drummer led a life to be envied, and the stories that followed in his wake were a tribute to him.

Jokes, anecdotes, and tall tales were told about the legendary exploits of the drummer, who was himself a joke teller and user of all the latest slang. The merchants enjoyed a good story, and a drummer always had a new one, because it was good for business. Freud wrote that "a new joke acts almost like an event of universal interest; it is passed from one person to another like the news of the latest victory . . . It is remarkable how universally popular a smutty interchange . . . is among common people and how it unfailingly produces a cheerful mood."[1] The cheerful mood, however, cloaked a good deal of hostility between the traveling drummer, who represented the urban dandy, and the farmer or small-town storekeeper, who was the rural sage. The theme of most of the jokes about drummers involved a game of one-upmanship between these representatives of two disparate ways of life.

A man named Alex E. Sweet addressed a convention of traveling men in Dallas in 1896 and gave an accurate self-image of the drummer as irresistible conqueror.

"The predominant trait of the drummer is what is called cheek, or gall, or both. The country merchant has no protection against the drummer. The commercial emissary disarms him with a smile, and in fifteen minutes tells the old man four good jokes, pays him five compliments on his business ability, propounds three conundrums, and perhaps comes near telling the truth once."[2]

A poem that appeared in the trade press reflected the status of the drummer with the front-porch crowd.

> I kind o' like to see 'em come,
>   They look so mighty smilin',
> They sorta liven up the town
>   And keep the pot a-bilin';

The landlord hurries in and out,
And has a brisker walk,
And all the loafers stand about
And grin to hear 'em talk.

To the buyer, the drummer was a bright spot in the day. T. J. Carey wrote: "I like his breezy ways, his unaffected and easy style of approach, the bits of news he brings me of trade changes and conditions, and the . . . insincere deferences (which never deceived, nor is it intended they should) that he seeks opportunity to ladle out. He is a newspaper-market report, funny column, society and police news, and all the rest of it, with editorials upon every page. He is a blessed nuisance; a pervading, invading, awakening influence with a mixed tendency to good and evil."[3]

A drummer's first pride was his persistence. In keeping with the American style of humor through exaggeration, the tenacity of the drummer was a popular source of yarns. In 1877, a character named Welkers appeared as *The Dry Good Drummer*. Welkers traveled across the country in a huge wagon accompanied by a brass band. He was indefatigable, resourceful, and aggressive without cynical reflection. Traveling west in a desolate country, Welkers met a sourdough sitting on a wretched old mule. He's busted. "Busted?" said Welkers, warming up. "Build a store. My friend, you look like a businessman. A businessman can't be busted. A man of energy and perseverance. Build a store and start a town right here. If there is a woman within two hundred miles of here, she'll find you if you've got dry goods to sell, and in no time town pumps will spring up around you, and hotels and gambling shops and private houses and gin mills, and everything else that goes toward making a comfortable and happy town; and you will be boss of all the corner lots to sell at five thousand dollars apiece. I offer you a fortune." And Welkers took his order for

$8000 worth of goods to be delivered in 30 days. And, we are told, the town thrived so in six months that they talked of sending the merchant to Congress.

That was what drummers did. They made towns blossom in the wilderness.

To the farm folks the persistence of the drummer was viewed less benignly. A farmer and his wife decided to buy a sewing machine and an organ, and before they even told anyone, they were set upon by agents, who came day and night: "And the fellers kep' a comin' and a goin' at all hours. For a spell, at first, Josiah would come in and talk with 'em, but after a while he got tired out, and when he would see one a comin' he would start on a run for the barn, and hide."[4]

The most persistent and ubiquitous drummer was the book agent. His tenacity was faithfully preserved in many jokes.

A man came out of an office building on the run and started down the street.

"Here! Here!" cried the policeman on the corner. "What's your hurry?"

'There's a man back there trying to sell me a book on twenty-eight weekly installments of two dollars and thirty-eight cents each!" cried the victim.

The policeman instantly released his hold.

"Run!" he cried. "Run like a whitehead!* Maybe you can get away from him yet."

One persistent drummer delayed a train robbery, declaring that he should retain 2 percent, since it was a cash transaction. When it was settled, the drummer had sold the robber a bill of burglar alarms, getting back his money, and taking a chattel mortgage for the balance.

Phrases abounded that sought to characterize the epitome of drummer determination: He could sell ivory letter openers to elephants. He could sell iceboxes to

* A type of torpedo developed in the late 1800s and noted for its great speed.

eskimos. He could sell framed copies of the Declaration
of Independence in England.

As confident and quick-witted as the traveling salesman was pictured, he had his vulnerabilities. While he
was out knocking on other people's doors, he apparently
gave more than a little thought to who might be knocking
on *his* door at home.

Long weeks, sometimes months, he was away from
home. Year after year. When he did get home, he was
exhausted. When he was away, his wife could think about
the many opportunities and temptations he'd have to
dally. Did she sit by the fire, alone, night after night,
keeping a faithful vigil? There are a few hundred jokes
that say she didn't.

A traveling salesman wired his wife that he would
be home that evening. When he arrived he found her in
another man's arms. He was despondent. His friends suggested that he talk it over with another woman, perhaps
his mother. The fellow consented. "Mother," he recounted,
as his eyes filled with tears, "I was out on the road selling.
Yesterday I wired my wife I'd be home last night, and
when I got home I found her in another man's arms. Why?
Mother, you're a woman. Tell me why?"

His mother was quiet for a long time. Finally she
broke the silence. "Maybe she didn't get your telegram."

In the early days of this century, a traveling man
wrote a piece that was only an exaggeration of the truth:
"I'm away so much that half the time I can't even remember my own address. I have to wire my firm from time to
time to find out where I live. At one time I was away so
long I actually forgot I was married. When I landed in a
strange town I fell in love with a beautiful woman and
married her. Fortunately, when I introduced her to my
boss he informed me that she was my wife before."

One little boy, the son of such a father as this, came
crying to his mother: "That red-headed guy who stays

here on Sunday licked me." (This joke first appeared in 1897, and last appeared, to my knowledge, in 1945.)

When the salesman was on the road, his most inspired adversary was not the buyer he had set out to snare, but the hayseeds and hicks he met along the way. They were opposite forces; common horse sense pitted against brass and cheek—the city slicker and the rube. The encounter between the traveling salesman and the farmer was of the classic Arkansas Traveler pattern. The original Arkansas Traveler was, according to tradition, Colonel Sandford C. Faulkner of Little Rock, who got lost in the mountains in 1840. He approached a log cabin and the squatter stubbornly evaded, or pretended to misunderstand, his questions. He offered to play a tune on the squatter's fiddle and afterwards was welcomed as a friend. Subsequent dialogues between harassed travelers and crotchety locals followed. Here is a dialogue pieced together out of drummer-farmer jokes.

"Hey, Hiram, which way to Pittstown?"
"How'd you know my name was Hiram?"
"Just guessed it."
"Then guess the way to Pittstown."

"Is that bull safe?"
"He's a durn sight safer'n you."

"I'm a sanitary engineer," said the bathtub drummer. "What are you doing to protect your family from the flu epidemic raging the country?"
"I bought a sanitary cup and we *all* drink from it."

"How much do you get for those potatoes?"
"Seventy-five cents a bushel."
"If you had them in New York, you could get a dollar and a half for them."
"Ya-as, and if I had a pail of water in hell, I reckon I could get ten cents a glass for it, too."

"Where does this road run?"

"Nowhere. It's been right there for nigh on to thirty years."

"You live all your life?" asked the salesman.
"Not yit."

"Not much difference between you and a fool is there?"

"No," said the farmer. "Just this fence."

"Why don't you want to buy this book?" asked the book agent.
"I don't like the way it's written."

"You never wrote a book and you presume to judge writing?"

"I never laid an egg, but I'm a better judge of omelets than any chicken in these parts."

"What you really need is this fine bicycle."
"I got only enough money to buy a cow."

"But think how funny you'll look riding to town on a cow."

"Not half as funny as I'll look trying to milk that bicycle."

The cool reception the traveling man got from the farmer was matched by others outside the cities who objected to fancy dudes.

Eastern salesmen traveling in Texas got rough treatment from the place and the people. One drummer said that when he got off the train his hat blew away, and while he was chasing his hat his trunk blew away. "Everything that grows has a thorn, and everything that breathes, stings."

A cowboy saw a fancy drummer standing at the bar and rode his horse right up to the bar next to him. Another cowboy, seeing the joke, rode up on the other side of the drummer. When the traveling man complained to the bartender, he just growled at him, "What you doin' in here afoot, anyhow?"

Aside from the time he spent selling and talking to the farmers who leaned on fences, the drummer spent most of his time in hotels and restaurants, and on trains. And there, too, he met his old sparring mate:

"The swell drummer on the train had just finished his morning toilet, carefully put his Cashmere Bouquet soap, his manicure set, and his powder box in his alligator gilt-edged satchel. He left his toothbrush to one side of the wash basin, and was adjusting his puff scarf and four-carat diamond when a frowzy-looking hayseed with a red undershirt entered, removed a big quid of tobacco from his mouth, took a dive into the basin, and wiped his face. He espied the drummer's toothbrush and immediately began to scrub his teeth. The drummer turned around to finish his make-up. He missed the brush, and looked in astonishment at the countryman making good use of it.

"Holy smoke!" he shouted. "Stranger, that's my toothbrush."

"Well, I swan! I thought it belonged to the car."[5]

Although trains were in use as early as 1834, it was not until the 1860s that the major cities were connected, and Pullman cars were not used until 1864.

The railroad transformed the shape and thought of America. In 1800, a trip to St. Louis from New York took six weeks. In 1857, the same trip could be made in three days. Diaries of travelers in the days before railroads reveal a curious patience with the delays of only a day or so. The anecdotes and jokes of the railroad travelers reveal a sharp impatience with delays running over an hour.

Up to the time of the First World War, the train was still, for most Americans, a pretty exotic form of transportation. Jokes tend to thrive on novelty, and traveling-salesman jokes, through the first decade of this century, were mostly stories involving the drummer in conflict with traveling farmers (continuing the urban-rural clash), conductors, porters, newsboys, old maids in the sleeping car, and food. A vaudeville song celebrated the fare a drummer was likely to get when he ventured into the railway station in search of something to eat:

The old railroad sandwich, the iron-bound sandwich,
The fly-covered sandwich that sets on the shelf.
How oft in the days when I worked as a drummer,
Have I at some crossing jumped off for a meal.
And seeing the sandwich proceeded to put it
Where moths couldn't harm it and thieves couldn't
    steal . . .[6]

Eating *on* a train could be a pleasant experience, and on prestige trains such as the Pioneer Limited the dining-car steward for fifty years was an Irishman named Dan Healy, who enjoyed wide fame among traveling men. After his place had been taken by a younger man, a magazine ran a sentimental editorial declaring that the ghost of the famed Healy should not obscure the excellence of the new man.

What drummers remembered most about the railroad was its slow pace. It was a favorite subject for smoking-car stories.

A conductor asked a drummer for his ticket. The man insisted that he had given the conductor his ticket at Wingo Junction. "Why," said the conductor, "only a little boy got on at Wingo Junction." "Yes," said the drummer, "I'm that little boy."

"Don't argue with me," said the conductor. "I've been on this line twenty years."

"My God," said the drummer, "what station did you get on at?"

The drummer asked the conductor what the delay was.

"A cow on the track," he replied.

"I thought that cow was chased off an hour ago."
"Yes, but we caught up with it again."

As the trains crossed and recrossed America, people heard of towns and cities with strange names. The relative speed of the train, as compared to the stage and riverboat, was drawing the country together, and people became fascinated with the names of their new neighbors.

Traveling men were particularly fond of talking about the strange-sounding places they had been to:

> Jargon like this his ears would fill—
> Kennebec and Boabil
> Kalamazoo and Waakesha;
> Wausion and Omaha,
> Muscogee and Kankadee.

A good deal of humor was aroused by the sleeping car, where strangers of all sizes and sexes were bedded down in uppers and lowers. It was perfect situation comedy:

The drummer was in the upper, happily snoring away. The old maid was in the lower, unable to sleep because of the rumbling. Finally she got her shoe and furiously rapped on the upper berth. "You can tap all night, lady," the drummer said, "but I ain't coming down."

Probably one of the oldest sleeping-car jokes concerned the traveling salesman who found the roach in his berth and wrote a letter to the president of the railroad complaining that he traveled a lot and felt that the railroad had displayed a shocking laxity in maintaining sanitary accommodations for the traveling public. He received a solicitous letter from the president expressing his profound regret. Clipped to the letter was a memo his assistant had obviously neglected to remove. It was a penciled note reading, "John, send this son of a bitch the bug letter."

Another sleeping-car anecdote of long life (1896–1939)* is about a drummer who told the porter to wake him at 5:30 A.M. and get him off the train in Detroit, even if he had to do it forcibly. "I might give you a struggle, because I like to sleep late." The next morning the drummer woke up at 9:00 and found himself still on the train. He stormed down the corridor to find a somewhat battered porter who was surprised to see him. "Good Lord, I wonder who I put off the train in Detroit?"

Many of the jokes produced about his accommodations, food, and travel were exaggerated laments.

The traveling salesman was freezing in bed and finally went down to complain to the manager. Just then an old doctor out on a night call saw the light on in the hotel and came in out of the storm. Snow stood on his shoulders and icicles dripped from his beard. "My God," said the salesman, "what room did *he* have?"

Another drummer went to the front desk to leave a wake-up call. "Never mind," said the clerk. "We get everybody up at six, so we can use the sheets for tablecloths."

Just as a traveler was writing his name on the register of a Leavenworth hotel, a bedbug appeared and made its way across the page. The man paused and remarked:

"I've been bled by St. Joe fleas, bitten by Kansas City spiders, and interviewed by Fort Scott graybacks; but I'll be darned if I was ever in a place before where the bedbug looked over the hotel register to find out where your room was."

A hotel for commercial travelers in Oklahoma posted these rules:

"Gents goin' to bed with their boots on will be charged extra.

"Three raps at the door means there is a murder in the house and you must get up.

---

* I recently heard this on a television talk show.

"Please write your name on the wallpaper so we know you've been here."

Probably the most famous of the traveling-salesman jokes involving a hotel concerned the drummer who checked in late at night. The night clerk warned him that the man in the room below was extremely nervous. The drummer retired to his room and began to undress for bed. He dropped one shoe loudly to the floor, then remembering the nervous man downstairs, put the other shoe down quietly. Just as he was falling asleep, there was a hammering at the door. It was his nervous neighbor. "When in the hell are you going to drop that other shoe?"

The "wrong room" was always a good situation for humor, and there were many versions of it.

A traveling man in a small-town hotel felt a sudden call to use the toilet in the middle of the night. He hastened down the hall to the door he thought opened into the toilet. It was locked. In a few minutes he tried again. Again he found it locked. Again he waited, until he could stand it no longer, and a third time went down the hall, only to find the door still locked. The door he had been trying led, not to the toilet, but to a room which that night was occupied by a bridal couple. Inside, the groom had been getting nervous under the repeated interruptions, so when he heard the doorknob turn a third time, he shouted gruffly: "What do you want?" "You ought to know," came the traveling man's voice from without. "If you ain't using both holes in there, I want one."[7]

Mistaken identity was a cause of trouble when one traveling salesman checked into his favorite hotel only to find it under new management. He was assured that service would be as good as ever. "Fine. Then send a woman up to my room as usual." The new manager's wife heard about this request and adamantly objected to her husband. "Okay, then *you* tell him," said the husband.

She went storming up the stairs to tell the salesman that this was a decent hotel and there would be no such goings on. After a few minutes there was a terrible commotion, and the manager went to see what had happened. He was greeted by the salesman, face scratched and shirt torn. "That was a tough old bird you sent," he said, "but, by God, I made her."

The restaurant provided an ideal place for the drummer to display his wit. In the restaurant he was at odds with the waiter, flirted with the waitress, and complained about the food. Here is a dialogue made up of restaurant jokes.

Drummer: "I'll have fly specks."
Waitress: "We don't serve them."
Drummer: "Then take them off the menu."

To Waitress: "What's your name?"
Waitress: "Pearl."
Drummer: "Ah, pearl of great price."
Waitress: "No, pearl cast before swine."

Drummer (dining with his wife): "Waiter, where's my chicken?"
Waiter (in loud whisper): "She doesn't work here any more."

Drummer: "It's a nice day, isn't it?"
Waitress: "Yes, it is, and so was yesterday and the day before, and I know I'm a pretty girl and have lovely blue eyes and I've been here quite a while and I like the place and my wages are satisfactory and there isn't a show or dance in town and if there were I would go alone. I'm from the country and I'm respectful and my brother is a college graduate and is the cook of this hotel and weighs three hundred pounds—now what'll you have, roast beef, roast pork, liver, hamburger, or Irish stew?"

Drummer: "Oh give me a bottle of milk and put a nipple on it."

A type of joke and anecdote popular with drummers concerned their relationships with the H.O. (home office). The sales manager at the home office usually expected salesmen to spend less money, make more calls, try harder, get more sales.

The attitude of the home office was characterized in the joke about the drummer who died on the road. His office received a wire from the local sheriff asking for instructions. The H.O. wired back: "Search through the clothes and see if he had any orders."

Another salesman wired his firm: "Saw Marshall Field today. No orders but a feather in my cap." Later he wired: "Saw Rothman today, no orders, but a feather in my cap." And so it went as the salesman traveled across the country. When he reached the last stop in California, he received a wire from his sales manager: "Remove feathers from cap. Make wings. Fly home. Firm bankrupt, cannot send carfare." This joke has different versions about what the salesman can do with the feathers.

From Cincinnati a salesman sent in his expense account, containing the item, "One isn't made of wood —$10. Later from Indianapolis, his expense account read, "One isn't made of wood—$35." When he received the third expense account with "One isn't made of wood— $45," the sales manager wired back, "One isn't made of steel, either."

The most popular traveling-salesman jokes remembered today are about the farmer's daughter, whose seduction by the city drummer may be considered symbolic of the ascendency of the urban over the rural as the second industrial revolution wore on.

It is interesting that the jokes about the traveling salesman and the farmer's daughter are based on actual

events that took place in the 1700s. Travelers in the
colonies sought refuge in any cabin or farmhouse they
happened to pass as night came upon them. The obliging
family usually put an extra plate on the table and made
room in bed. Much has been written about bundling, or
bed-sharing. The practice was widespread, originating in
Europe, and maintained in America according to where
the settlers of a region came from.

Bundling was a ritual of courtship in parts of New
England and Pennsylvania, and later in Ohio. But when
strangers were given refuge for the night, it was occasionally the practice to put them in bed with the children. In America, bundling was practiced in sparsely
settled areas where there were no taverns or inns, or
where they were overcrowded, as was often the case.
From the diaries of early travelers, it is apparent that
some naïveté existed which would echo through the cen-
turies in countless jokes.

There were tinkers, grinders, peddlers, preachers, circuit judges, book agents, musicians, poets, and assorted
characters who wandered across the land and slept with
the farmer's daughter, but it was with the traveling salesman that her name was to be forever linked. The first
wholesale drummer inherited the reputation, but it is
not likely that he enjoyed her favors. The average commercial went on the train, with a 200-pound trunk riding in freight. He was not likely to show up at a remote
farmhouse looking for a place to spend the night. Of
course, when the automobile came into general use, flat
tires and empty gas tanks renewed the nocturnal pil-
grimage to the farmhouse, at least in jokes.

Two of the more well-worn of the farmer's-daughter
jokes had previous lives as bundling jokes. After having
been told he could spend the night but would have to
sleep with the daughter, the traveling salesman is warned
not to cross a narrow bolster which has been placed in
the middle of the bed. The next morning he is walking

around the farmyard before breakfast and starts to climb over a fence. The farmer's daughter tells him to be careful. "Anyone who can't climb over a pillow will break his neck on that fence."

In the other joke, the traveling salesman is told that he must sleep on top of the sheet and that the farmer's daughter will stay under the sheet. Several years later he revisits the farm and notices an undersized boy playing in the yard. The man inquires about the boy's small stature and is told, "You'd be runty too, if somebody strained you through a sheet."

In both of these stories, the restrictions placed on the traveling salesman, i.e., the pillow and the sheet, were part of the practice of courtship bundling. The first story appears in various jokebooks as a salesman joke and as a bundling joke. The practice of bundling preceded traveling salesmen in history, and so claims title.

It is not clear when these bundling jokes were changed to traveling-salesman jokes, but updating is a common practice, and once done, it attracted parodies which were not associated with bundling. For example: The traveling salesman asked to spend the night in the farmhouse, but only the farmer's wife was home. She decided to take a chance and showed him to the guest room. He couldn't stop thinking about her and found it impossible to sleep. Then came a sudden soft tap at the door. "Would you like company?"

"You bet your life I would," he shouts.

"That's fine," the lady replied. "You see, another gentleman whose car broke down is at the door and wants me to put him up."

Few new jokes about traveling salesmen were heard after the turn of the century. The jokes that were printed could be traced back to an earlier time. Now traveling men were changing, business was changing, the times were changing.

People joke about what matters to them, and to a

fickle public the drummers didn't matter so much any
more. Twentieth-century man wasn't going to experience
the world vicariously.

In 1937, S. D. Mann, a traveling salesman, described
his bleak life on the road—fifteen years of struggling with
sample cases, eating alone or with another salesman, sleeping in tiny hotel rooms. He ended his article, "We don't
live to be too old, we traveling salesmen. Life is too
hectic, too irregular. We are under too much pressure
and strain to stand it for many years . . . 'Have you
heard the one about the traveling salesman?' From com-
rade, chance acquaintance, radio, newspaper, stage,
screen, the question comes. Smile, listen, then laugh,
for its bound to be a good one, even tho it's not true to
life. Commercial slaves, that's what we are, chained to a
treadmill from which we wouldn't escape if we could,
but the world pays us its tribute for being one of its best
stock mediums, for universal jest and humor.

"So laugh, please! Thank you."[8]

Although the traveling-salesman joke is dead, I occasionally hear some of these same stories on television,
altered a little, and presented fresh to audiences who
probably are too young to remember.

Chapter Four

The Turn
of the Screw

Beginning in the last few years of the nineteenth century, the life of the traveling salesman became more hectic. Drummers found themselves spending more time going after business and less time developing the finer points of their life style. Rapid economic expansion and a growing need to dispose of the goods that new factories were pouring out led business managers to look for ways to increase their sales. Most of the ways they found resulted in pressure on the salesman in the field and a certain encroachment on his assumed rights as commercial prima donna.

T. J. Carey described the traveling man of 1899 as an autocrat. "He selects the most central part of the office, and there he spreads forth his samples and scatters his belongings in an ever widening radius. Old letters and printed matter he files upon the floor. The man who is the busiest is the one he must consult immediately upon some important point . . . He badgers the superintendent and contradicts him as the manager himself would hesitate to do, disregards or openly flouts all the rules of the office, and under his example the office discipline falls into a state of demoralization that takes a week or two to reform . . . for is he not the man who brings the trade, whose progress from town to town is watched with anxious care, whose big, fat letters with the orders . . . bring joy?"[1]

This was the concept of the salesman as the grand drummer, and it was outdated when these words were written. Competition in the marketplace was becoming more intense. It was clear that modern industry needed a sales force that could be controlled as efficiently and productively as the lines of humming and clanking machines. Drummers were going to have to keep up with the realities of the assembly line. The potential of mass production gave assurance that shortages of goods—in any real sense—would no longer be a reliable ally to the salesman.

Buried in this reality was a madness that seemed to have seized men who ran the factories. If so many products *could* be produced, then so many products *should* be produced, and therefore would *have* to be sold. The study of commercial history leaves one with the impression that great factories grew not because they were needed, but because they were possible. The constant barrage directed at the average citizen today to buy something came into being for reasons not fully explained by greed, necessity, or economics. It developed more to accommodate the fascination with production. Had production risen solely as a response to demand—as classic economic theory insists—then there would be no salesmen. Ironically, modern methods of selling grew out of the development of a product for which there was no demand, and a great deal of opposition—that is, the cash register.

John Henry Patterson was not only the champion of the cash register but also the man who put salesmen in step with production. He had as severe a case of production madness as has ever been recorded.

Before Patterson's day, it was usual to give a new salesman a little talk before he went on the road for the first time—perhaps a few words of encouragement to do the best he could. If he sold a reasonable amount of goods, nobody bothered him. No one dreamed of trying to tell him how to sell. Patterson so dreamed, however, and to the old-line drummers his dream was a nightmare.

John Patterson had been a coal dealer in Dayton, Ohio, before he bought out the National Manufacturing Company in 1884 and changed its name to the National Cash Register Company. Neither James Ritty, the man who invented the cash register, nor his successor had been able to sell enough machines to keep the business going. Patterson had sold his coal business and had cash and time on his hands. His offer to buy out the new company was readily accepted. Only after the papers were signed did Patterson learn that the company was a standing joke in Dayton. The prospects of the cash register were so dismal that Patterson tried to sell the company back at a loss, and discovered that he couldn't give it away. He settled down, somewhat grimly, to the task of acquainting the world with the cash register.

Ritty's cash register was a simple machine that punched holes in a roll of paper. By counting up the holes, the storekeeper could find out how much money had been rung up for the day. Patterson made a few improvements on the machine and turned his attention to sales. The success he achieved not only built the company, but completely altered the selling process and the lives of the salesmen involved in it.

It was the traditional practice of bartenders and store clerks of the day to pocket a portion of the day's receipts out of the open cash drawer. With no record of how much money the drawer should contain, it was not difficult to raid the till. Patterson's attention had been called to the cash register when he had operated a store near one of his coal mines. He did a brisk business at his own prices, yet each year the store lost money. The installation of one of Ritty's Incorruptible Cash Registers allowed the store to begin showing a profit.

Patterson was a firm believer in the new machine and claimed with evangelical fervor that "the jails of the world are full of victims of the open cash drawer." The clerks and bartenders who were the object of his concern were unimpressed. To them, the cash register was an ornate accusation of thievery and a monumental symbol of the owner's lack of faith, demeaning the employee's integrity in the eyes of his customers. The cash register was originally advertised as a "thief catcher," a term that equally outraged the honest clerks and aproned thieves confronted with one of Patterson's brass gadgets.

Direct mail was aimed at storekeepers with tireless regularity. Patterson was one of the first systematic users of direct-mail advertising, and he used it to a degree that bordered on persecution. A bewildered storekeeper returned a flier from one of Patterson's energetic campaigns with a penciled note: "Let up. We never done you no harm."[2]

Store employees quickly learned to pick out the envelopes from NCR and fire them into the nearest trash can. Patterson tried sending out his advertisements in plain brown envelopes. The clerks discarded every piece of mail postmarked from Dayton, whereupon Patterson had his mail sent from all over the state.

An NCR salesman calling on a store or saloon was likely to be thrown out before he had a chance to speak to the owner, and other traveling salesmen were quick to establish their innocence of the cash-register trade. The opposition was so strong that it almost resulted in the formation of a national clerks union.

Against this unpromising beginning, Patterson threw

what even his friendliest biographer called "his ruthless will."[3]

In his quest to make the cash register a standard fixture in every retail establishment, John Patterson originated many of the practices that have become fixtures in the modern sales office.

He got his salesmen together to discuss ways of combating the clerks' protective association and is credited with calling the first sales conference.

The annual sales meeting eventually became a huge convention where Patterson indulged his taste for showmanship. He used skits, often played by professional actors, to illustrate a selling situation. He had a crew of carpenters build realistic store sets and elaborate props to illustrate his sales talks. He was a great believer in the visual. The nerve from the eye to the brain was twenty-two times stronger than the nerve of the ear to the brain. He figured that 87 percent of what a man learned was learned through his eyes. Many of Patterson's eccentricities, for which he was famous, were richly and visually displayed at his sales conventions. To emphasize a point, he would stomp on his eyeglasses, smash a cash register to junk, kick in a desk, knock a water pitcher to the floor, or throw money.

It seemed inconsistent that a man with such a temperament should have quieted the style of the salesman, but he was concerned with the salesman's image, and he changed it. To the joke-telling drummer with the big cigar and the fancy clothes, the new image was total. "Don't tell funny stories," said Patterson, and when calling on a customer, "Don't smoke."

He did not want them to discuss the weather, the silver problem, or anything other than cash registers. Talk about people who have bought them, and people who need them. Talk about special features, talk about anything connected with cash registers.

He wanted his salesmen to dress well but not ex-

travagantly. He would round up a group of salesmen
and send them off to New York for several suits of well-
tailored clothes, but he would land on a salesman for
wearing a flashy necktie. Good clothes were an asset, but
sporty clothes were a distraction. Calendars and clocks
were, and still are, banned from NCR display rooms
for the same reason. He insisted that his salesmen wear
freshly starched collars, shined shoes, and be clean shaven
at all times.

In the beginning, he merely made suggestions to the
salesmen, but as he and "the Cash" grew stronger, his
suggestions became less optional. During the panic of
1893, the threat of a national financial crisis and prolonged depression provided Patterson with the opportunity
to enforce his suggestions with an iron hand.

One of the battles between Patterson and his salesmen was fought over the use of the sales primer. The sales
primer was the first canned sales talk—that is, it was
written down and committed to memory. Joseph Crane
was the most successful agent at the Cash, and when Patterson questioned him about how he sold he discovered
that Crane had worked out a presentation and used it on
every sale. Patterson had declared that a salesman was
made on earth and not created in heaven, and the
prospects of having a standard sales pitch delighted him.
He called in a secretary, and Crane dictated his memorized sales message. It was printed up in 1887 as *How
I Sell a National Cash Register*. To the drummer who depended on ready wit and personal charm, the book was
heresy, but in the troubled year of 1893 those who stayed
with the Cash learned it by heart and recited it to the
little tyrant from Dayton who toured the provinces
for that special purpose.

Two of Patterson's most profound changes in the
salesman's world was the institution of the guaranteed
territory and the quota system.

Patterson dismissed the "saturation theory," to the

consternation of those who feared that he would soon find no one who didn't own a cash register. Patterson believed that a given territory possessed a per capita sales potential that could be delivered every year, and should even increase with the population. He assigned the salesman to a specific territory, into which no others were allowed to trespass nor from which the salesman was allowed to wander. And he set a definite quota based on the amount of business the company expected. The salesman was judged not on his dollar volume but on his performance in relationship to his quota. A sales club was formed and membership was bestowed on those who sold 100 percent of their quota. Nonmembers did not long tarry in the cash-register business. Those who made it were well paid. One old-timer at the Cash said employees were overpaid and overpunished. Patterson believed that fear and greed were the principal motivating influences of most men.

To see to it that salesmen made their quotas, Patterson continued his heavy use of direct-mail advertising, set up a training school—the first, by the way—and established an Inventions Department to constantly dream up new features to be added to the latest model of the cash register. NCR salesmen were probably the first to systematically practice upgrading. Where most salesmen saw little need to waste time on people who had already bought their product, the cash-register men always had a new feature to talk about, and lists of old customers were as valuable to them as new prospects.

The confined territory and quota system brought about the first use of "intensive supervision" of field salesmen. The average drummer of the time saw little of his home office, and the sales manager's function was largely confined to keeping records. The traveling man sent his orders in to the house, and the house sent him his commissions. No orders, no commissions. But since Patterson viewed the territory in terms of its potential, or imagined,

worth, a salesman who wasn't doing his job was a loss
to the company. The salesman now found himself under
constant pressure to get more sales.

Thomas Wolfe devoted a chapter of *You Can't Go
Home Again* to describe the brutal way in which a district sales agent "managed" his agents in the territory
by threats and insults in private and a display of sunny
paternalism in public.

Something in this cynicism was inherent in the "contests" that became very popular under Patterson. Under
the edict of produce or perish, salesmen donned paper
jocky hats in a sales contest hailed as the "Great NCR
Derby." Each sales office used little cut-out horses to
show the standing of each salesman "jockey." A prize
was awarded to the jockey who amassed the most quota
points during the contest period. The company house
organ, *The Hustler,* carried a breathless account of the
race, couched in the language of the track and illustrated
with pictures of the leaders in each district. The whole
thing would have appalled E. P. Briggs.

If you had told those proud drummers of the nineteenth century that in a few years they would be parrot-
ing sales talks, marching around singing inspirational
sales songs, and trying to win prizes in sales contests,
they would have knocked you down.

The growth of NCR was not wholly attributable to
the superiority of either their salesmen or their cash
registers. William Rodgers,[4] in his unauthorized biography of IBM and the Watsons, brought to light the fas-
cinating story of how Patterson set about wiping out the
competition. By legal harassment, price cutting, bribery,
fist fights, vandalism, and industrial espionage, he thor-
oughly dominated the cash-register market.

Thomas J. Watson, Sr. as a young cash-register salesman had established himself as an up-and-comer in the
Rochester territory and was summoned to Dayton. He
was given a million dollars to set up an independent

corporation to deal in secondhand cash registers. His
assignment was to "knock out," drive out, or buy out all
the competition without revealing his association with
NCR.

In 1913, the U. S. Government brought suit against
Cash for violations of the antitrust law. A key Government witness was Hugh Chalmers, who had been the
number-two man at NCR. Chalmers was himself the archi-
tect of a good bit of the strategy that landed the company in court before he had been fired by Patterson.

The trial was quite a sensation, and the whole nation
followed the plots and intrigues of big business. The verdict was guilty on all counts. Patterson and Watson,
along with other company executives were sentenced to a
year in jail and fined $5000.

Patterson had not invented the cash register, but he
felt that he had at least discovered it, and in so doing
had a right over all the business. Now under threat of
prison, it appeared that a higher authority was about to
intercede on his behalf. The city of Dayton, whose
citizens had rather enjoyed the trials, was about to be
punished.

A fierce rainstorm swept across the town and held
its fury until the Mad and Miami rivers spread their waters
across Dayton, sparing only the Cash, which was perched
high and dry on a hill overlooking the disaster. Patterson
opened the factory to the citizens and put his carpenters
to work building rowboats. Food and medical supplies
were made available to all. Watson, in New York sent
a trainload of fresh supplies. The newspapers hailed Patterson as a hero.

When the waters parted, a new trial was granted on
a technicality, and a second trial was never begun. The
Government settled for a consent decree. Patterson had
by this time tired of Watson and fired him.

Patterson was a short man with a high, rasping
voice. He was an arrogant peacock with a pince-nez and

a handlebar mustache. He rode a white horse because
Napoleon had. He was an eccentric whose abberations
were a curious challenge to young men full of ambition. The more impossible he became, the more determined were the applicants for jobs at the Cash. He was
a poor judge of men, and was harsh and unfair in his
treatment of them. He would instantly fire a man who did
anything he thought was stupid. He would eventually
fire any man who became "indispensable." He fired the
best and the worst and kept the mediocre and made their
life a living hell. His penchant for clearing out the executive suites of NCR always left plenty of room at the
top, and the promise of rapid promotion attracted young
men from all over the country. It was said that he either
fired or promoted any man who caught his attention.

His exiled executives, referred to as "alumnus" by
company historians, presided over an astonishing number
of the biggest companies in America. He "graduated"
more executive talent in ten years than most companies
saw in a lifetime.

Few of the men he fired could have considered their
dismissal just or sane. When Patterson became obsessed
with diet and health, he became openly distrustful of
any man who used butter and pepper. He imposed his
latest theories on his reluctant underlings. He made
early-morning horseback riding compulsory because he
felt his men didn't get enough exercise. He started a cooking school for the wives of all NCR salesmen and executives. Attendance, of course, was mandatory.

At various times he fasted (37 days), followed
Fletcher's theories of mastication, and became a vegetar-
ian. He visited doctors all over the world, including Dr.
John Harvey Kellogg of corn flake fame, and spent some
time in his sanitarium. He took four or five baths a day
and was extremely particular about their temperature.
During one of his visits abroad he acquired a Cockney
calisthenics instructor and trainer named Charles Palmer,

who claimed insights into phrenology. Palmer became quite a power at the Cash. Executives with heads that displeased him were fired forthwith. A Patterson firing was not a quiet dismissal, but was usually angry and abrupt. Tension at the upper levels of management was kept rather high.

It was Patterson's habit to practice benevolence in the factory and malevolence with his executives and salesmen. He was a follower of George Pullman in the practice of industrial welfare and built well-lit, nicely landscaped factories, with hospitals and first-aid stations, locker rooms, free uniforms, proper ventilation and safety devices, company dining rooms, and country clubs.

Patterson either instigated or popularized the eagerness of the corporation to engage the family in company business. He held special meetings for salesmen's wives to tell them how they should help their husbands. Contest prizes usually appealed to the salesman's wife in the hopes that she would prod him to win it for her. He encouraged the development of expensive tastes—production madness in full flower. He would send a man to New York or Europe with instructions to take his wife and buy her an expensive gown and charge it to the company.

When the cash-register business fell off sharply in 1914, one of Patterson's strategies was to hold a convention for the wives. For five days he gave chalk talks and exhorted the women to get behind their men and help them double their earnings. The highlight of this "riot of enthusiasm," to use his own appraisal, was a play about how the good wife should act. In the first act, the bad wife nags her husband and complains when he has to travel or work late. The rest of the play outlined what Patterson felt was the proper attitude—one of single-minded devotion to the Cash. (She *insisted* that any social plans be immediately canceled if they interfered with an after-hours demonstration of the cash register.)

The company was family enough for those who toiled for the Cash. He recalled that in the farmhouse of his childhood his mother "had nursed the hired men and cared for them just as though they had belonged to her . . . The factory has now taken the place of the old farm . . ."[5] And he had taken the place of Mother.

Patterson did not marry until he was forty-four, and his wife lived only six years, bearing him two children. He turned them over to his sister to bring up. He experienced very little family life and never got to know his children until they were grown. He had no time for them, and the life style he evolved for his salesmen and executives assured them that they would have little time for theirs. His successor was a humorless tyrant named Barringer, who "kept the organization in turmoil and whipped the sales force."[6] He worked from early morning to late at night in a single-minded devotion to the Cash that he expected of everyone else.

Stanley Allyn, a longtime NCR president and lifetime associate of Patterson, admitted that when he learned of Patterson's death he felt only a great sense of relief.[7]

By the time Patterson died, in 1922, his ideas about selling had been generally adopted by American industry and had spread around the world.

No more appropriate symbol than the cash register can be found for the Americanization of European salesmen and businessmen. The Cash began to be established abroad even while the Dayton factory was struggling to meet the weekly payroll. In 1896, the first international sales conference was held. Prior to 1895, European sales were handled by a few agents, and substantial sales were made only in England, Germany, Holland, and Italy. Patterson took a more direct interest in foreign business. NCR expanded into Vienna, Brussels, Madrid, and Prague. By 1908, NCR had penetrated the Balkans and entered Rumania, Bulgaria, Russia, Turkey, and Greece.

In the North, agencies were opened in Denmark, Sweden, and Switzerland.

NCR equipment now sells all over the world, with gross sales running over $523 million.

Today, we can see the many specific contributions John Patterson made to the theory and practice of selling, and to the general madness of the industrialized time in which we live.

The drummer of the 1800s may have been concocted of brass and cheek, but his life revolved around a spirit of adventure, personal pride, and good cigars. But by the curious standards of our more sophisticated century, Patterson's nerve-jangling jungle of training classes and quota points gave the traveling salesman's job a little more respect. It made it seem a little more scientific, more substantial, than the drummer.

In a magazine story in 1911, a young traveling salesman had proposed to his girl, and she rejected him because of his "line of work." Hotly, he protests that she is "sizing up the fraternity by the old-fashioned, hard-drinking drummer whose long suit was his ability to tell funny stories. I tell you, little girl, a fellow of that sort wouldn't stand the ghost of a chance nowadays. Modern salesmanship is conducted on scientific principles."[8]

An unlikely speech, but he got the girl.

Chapter Five

The Well-tuned Salesman

Selling was becoming an organizational effort presided over by managers. By the 1920s, no selling organization was complete without a sales manager to badger, cajole, reward, and punish his salesmen in the field.

Between the turn of the century and the First World War, the sales manager became an important figure in the business world. This was a fundamental change from the past, when selling had been largely a salesman's story. The legends of business were filled with the exploits of individuals who performed spectacular feats of single-handed salesmanship. Many of these are familiar: Heinz and his horseradish; Deere and the plow; Baldwin and the organ; Wilcox and plated silverware. The saga of the hero salesman made interesting reading, but it was becoming apparent that new marketing methods were needed to dispose of the goods that the factories were capable of turning out.

The sales managers of the 1800s were really office

managers whose function—as far as sales were concerned
—was to keep track of the traveling men, record how
much they sold, and see if they were paid.

Sanders Norvell was one of the first sales managers
to take a strong hand in establishing the sales manager's
corporate authority. The man he worked for, first as a
traveling salesman and then as a manager, was E. C.
Simmons, famous in the trade for having sent out the
first hardware drummers before the Civil War.

In 1888, Norvell was a traveling salesman in
Colorado during the mining boom. Unknown to Simmons,
Norvell opened an office and a showroom and trained a
force of salesmen. When Simmons stopped in for a visit,
he was amazed at what his young salesman had done.
Shortly afterward, Norvell was called back to St. Louis
and made General Sales Manager, a job he found frustrating for a number of reasons. He earned less money on
straight salary than he did on commission. He found
that he was expected to entertain the traveling men when
they were in town and join a few good clubs for business
reasons, all at his own expense. In addition to this,
company executives ignored him and wrote directly to
the traveling men about any matter that concerned them.
His predicament was not unusual. The job of sales
manager was new in the world, and the authority of
the position was not established.

Within a few years, Norvell had staked out his territory within the executive domain. He later became vice-
president and heir apparent, but instead went on to form
his own company, which was quite successful, increasing
sales by a million dollars a year for ten years. He retired
twice, returning to head McKesson & Robbins, and later,
Remington Arms. He was a prolific writer on the subject
of salesmanship and was widely quoted and interviewed.

The first book on sales management was written in
1913, but the idea of managing traveling salesmen was

greeted with incredulity. "Anybody can stick pins in a map, but whoever managed a force of traveling men?"[1]

The traveling man was still a pretty independent character, being one of God's best creations, or so he was told by a state senator from Illinois at the annual convention of the National Association of Traveling Men in 1913. A few years later, Woodrow Wilson would address the National Council of Traveling Men, another of the many travelers' groups, to tell them how important they were to international trade and understanding among nations.

As the sales manager improved his own standing within the corporate structure, his attitude toward his salesmen began to resemble that of a professor toward undergraduates, with all the positive and negative aspects inherent in that comparison. When *Sales Management* asked a group of sales managers what they thought was the most important element in managing a sales force, all but one saw himself as a leader and teacher of men. They identified their jobs in terms of "knowing your men," developing loyalty, keeping up morale, making better men of them, and "training youngsters." Only one sales manager saw his job in terms of the consumer, whom he felt should be provided with the greatest value at the least cost.[2]

The sales manager assumed for himself a certain omnipotence and grandly accepted credit or blame for the success or failure of his men. One sales manager said, in reference to the high dropout rate among new salesmen: ". . . we sales managers are to blame for it. We spoil these youngsters. We put the wrong ideas into their heads. We are either too sympathetic or too tolerant. . . . This softens and gives them a wrong idea of conditions in general."[3] Not many salesmen would have recognized that situation.

Sales managers were often divided in their opinions of the old-time salesmen, who took too much time talking to the customers, and the kids out of college. The sales manager, a professional malcontent, often complained about both. The modern salesman, grumbled one manager, is "getting soft and lacks ability and energy."[4] It was time to tighten up these youngsters and give them a taste of real work. *Sales Management* agreed with him and said managers were not as demanding of their salesmen as they were of themselves when they were on the road. Elsewhere in the same issue, an editorial gave tacit approval of the practice of firing older salesmen, who often were earning good money, and replacing them with younger men who would work for less. While the editors had "great respect for the salesman who had grown gray in sales work," he was a "great liability."[5] Thus did the view from this height reveal the young salesmen to be soft and the old salesmen to be a liability.

It was quite common to hear derogatory remarks about the older salesman's "personality" selling, which came to be so symbolized by the big handshake that the head buyer of a Chicago department store put a sign on his office door forbidding traveling salesmen to shake hands with him, an activity he considered a "mock gesture and as silly as rubbing noses."[6]

The First World War delayed the full flowering of managed salesmanship. The war took a great part of factory production, and many salesmen had relatively little selling to do. A gathering of sales managers was likely to center on what to do with the salesmen, rather than how to get them to sell. Some salesmen were put to work in the office or on the loading platform.

The major impact of America's capacity for overproduction was felt after the war, although according to J. R. Sprague, a frequent writer on salesmanship, there were signs of change before then. "High-powered salesmanship is comparatively modern," he wrote in 1931. "When I first went into business, salesmanship was a rather passive matter. When I retired, salesmanship was

almost as high-powered as it is now. I would name 1913
as the date at which modern high-powered salesmanship
first came to be employed on a large scale."[7]

An official of the U. S. Commerce Department, in
speaking of this era some years later, said "free deals,
secret discounts, missionary salesmen, and a thousand
and one other sales devices were used *to get rid* of the
ever expanding plant production."[8] (My italics.) This
was no cynical appraisal but a statement of fact. With the
full development of mass production, the salesman's job
changed considerably in its basic emphasis from the comparatively gentlemanly selling of the past to the frantic
imperative of getting rid of excess production.

We had arrived at what was described as the Marketing Age,[9] as America's ability to produce far out-
stripped her desire to consume. (Marketing, which
sounded like a more respectable activity than mere selling, was the attempt to stimulate demand for goods on a
broad basis.)

Stuart Chase called the postwar years the Age of the
Salesman. "Hence . . . sales quotas, the shattering of sales
resistance, the discovery of Jesus of Nazareth as the first
advertising man, courses on the development of personality, pie charts, maps with red, orange, and violet pins,
closing men, contact men, sucker lists, paint-up week,"
etc.[10] The big sell was already beginning to grate on the
public nerve.

E. J. Goodspeed, observing with dismay the "army
of trained, successful salesmen," wondered what the
prospects were "for the untrained, unsuccessful public.
What about us? Are we just to buy and buy and buy,
world without end?"[11] Another writer suggested that
since there were schools in the art of extracting money,
there should be someone to teach the art of holding on to
it. Clarence Darrow and Dr. John A. Stevenson, president
of the Equitable Life Assurance Society, debated the
value of the "modern" Babbitt type of "energetic sales-

manship" in 1925. Dr. Stevenson said it was a service and blessing to mankind. Mr. Darrow said it was bunk. Unfortunately, no record has survived of the debate.

The sales manager's job was to tune up the sales force, and his responsibility was to the company, not to the public's sensibilities. Sprague wrote about a meeting he had with a sales manager who was up on all the latest methods. "He talked enthusiastically of sales quotas, of dominating the prospect, breaking down sales resistance, and so forth. He called the two hundred traveling men his 'sizzling sales force' and he kept them sizzling by sending each one an abusive weekly letter."[12]

The sales manager tinkered with his sales department like a man learning to drive a Model T, trying to find what combination of actions made the thing run.

Business magazines were filled with suggestions and ideas about how to control salesmen, how to find the mainspring that makes a salesman go, how to encourage salesmen to organize their time, how to use sentiment, how to use the salesman's ego, how to hold the young salesman in line. They learned how to redesign their salesmen, how to let the salesman unburden his mind, how to make him worry a bit, how not to bear down too hard, and how to give first aid to the downhearted salesman. They learned two ironclad rules to keep sales up, ten plans for putting new life into a sales force, the big three for sales planning, seven master keys of sales management, five essentials and five pointers for good personal salesmanship, a hundred and one things to check salesmen for, three qualities that build salesmen, and a two-way plan for adding volume. This is only a sampling of what appeared in print during 1926 and 1927.

The most crucial adjustment performed upon the well-tuned salesman was the ongoing dickering with his quota and his territory. Quotas were not always set according to what might reasonably be gotten out of a territory. They more commonly reflected whatever sales volume the company needed or wanted, often ignoring market conditions and information readily available from trade associations.[13] The quota had one unvarying characteristic. This year's was bigger than last year's.

The sales quota was not only a directive to salesmen telling how much they would sell, it was a notice to the public of how much they would buy. Europeans thought the idea was absurd and insisted that such effrontery would cause a revolution if they tried it. Many Americans were equally opposed to the nation's obsession with selling. A survey made in 1931 found that a majority of those questioned felt that "a chief cause of crime is money madness, caused by commercialization of all life's activities."[14] The Ford Motor Company was held by some to be largely responsible for high-pressure selling in the automobile industry. Ford dealers had such stiff quotas that they resorted to door-to-door selling to sell enough cars to keep their dealerships.

In 1929, Sprague wrote a warning about the shrill tone of overselling that he saw intruding itself into the orderly and ethical conduct of business. High-pressure selling was, he said, "dangerous to the entire structure of American business. . . . Let the day arrive when enough Americans believe business is assuming the role of tyrant and business of all kinds will suffer, the innocent with the transgressor."[15] He was ignored, but the day may soon arrive.

Many companies had bad experiences with the quota system and lost some of their best salesmen, who felt that quota plans were "driving tactics to squeeze every ounce of work out of them." In fact, the intent of most quota plans was to stimulate competition among salesmen so that they could be "played against each other."[16]

To avoid the worst aspects of enforced quotas, American Multigraph and Burroughs Adding Machines favored a "profit sharing" plan, devised during the First World War to spur the salesmen on during a time when it was comparatively easy for them to increase sales, but still not take full advantage of all the potential business. The salesmen were paid a 20 percent commission on all sales below their quota, and a 25 percent commission on sales above their quota. The extra 5 percent was the salesman's share of the extra profit earned by the company on his sales.

The sales manager in the business-machines industry expected his men to earn $1800 a year. If a salesman's commission was less than that, he might well be fired. Most of them did quite well. In 1917, one addressing-machine salesman sold over $160,000 worth of equipment.

The sales manager controlled his men by adjusting their quotas, allocating territories, and selecting a compensation plan. The manager's control over these crucial variables rendered the most rebellious salesman attentive to the inspirational letters, lectures, meetings, and sales contests.

Most sales managers disliked straight commission because it weakened their hold on the salesman. "The big difficulty with the commission system lies in the fact that you cannot control the salesman. In other words, salesmen are not sales managers. If the salesman could sales-manage himself, then he could work on commission and make more money than he could on salary. But the trouble is that the salesman hasn't the nerve and hasn't the discipline to sales-manage himself. He needs a sales manager to help him."[17]

The net result of the sales manager's help as far as the traveling man was concerned, was that his territory got smaller, his quota bigger, his paper work longer, and his work harder. A good deal of resentment was created between the manager and the managed. In many cases the sales manager had never covered a territory himself, and his knowledge of the day-to-day problems was incomplete. One instance will serve to illustrate. The son of the founder of the company had just become president.

He was also acting as sales manager, and in going over the sales records he couldn't understand why his salesmen weren't selling more. He called in one of the salesmen and told him to get his samples and make a sales presentation. At the end of his sales spiel, the young president was greatly impressed with the salesman's delivery. "I can't understand it," he said. "That is irresistible."

The salesman said it was impossible for him to understand because he had never been out selling. He suggested that the president take the samples and make a presentation to him. Somewhat reluctantly, the young man took the samples and approached the desk to demonstrate his own sales technique. The salesman let him stand there for a minute before looking up. Then he shouted, "Get out! Get out, now! Get out before I put you out. John, come in and put this drummer out!" The president, flustered by this reception, objected strongly to being spoken to that way. The salesman told him that that was the kind of man he contended with every day.[18]

A good part of the time, the traveling man communicated with the sales manager by mail. Paper work caused a great deal of unhappiness among salesmen and some concern among managers, one of whom remarked that, in his opinion, salesmen were born and bookkeepers were made, and it was all too easy to make a bookkeeper out of a good salesman. One salesman complained that he had covered his territory for thirteen years and had only Sundays at home. He particularly resented the fact that he spent most of that day catching up on his paper work.

Most traveling salesmen sent in weekly, or even daily, call reports and expense accounts.

The expense account was a matter of constant concern to sales managers. Dartnell[19] surveyed managers in twenty different types of businesses and found in all of them a strong desire to reduce the salesman's traveling expenses. Various attempts were made to hold them down. A wholesaler in Birmingham, Alabama, tried to keep a continual record of the relationship between what a salesman spent and what he earned for the company. He used a calculating machine to prepare daily totals on all his salesmen, showing what they earned, what they spent, how much they sold, and what percentage of the company's business they accounted for. He compared each of these items with thirty days ago, sixty days ago, ninety days ago, and a year ago. It was felt that under this statistical spotlight the salesman would be more careful with the firm's money.

Some companies surveyed by Dartnell paid a per diem allowance ranging from $3.50 to $7. The addressing-machine salesmen, among the more aggressive travelers of the day, had an unlimited expense account, but they averaged a modest $5 a day in town and $4 on the road. This was exceeded by salesmen of filing equipment, corsets, engineering specialties, and hot water heaters, who averaged half again as much.

One large auto-supply company gave its men a salary of $1800 a year, but no commissions were paid until the amount due exceeded the saleman's travel expenses.

Entertainment expenses were, in some cases, limited to 5 percent of the salesman's salary. Two hundred and seven companies surveyed in 1917, which formerly had had "wide open" policies, all indicated a concern about the cost of entertaining. Fifty of the companies had adopted a "no entertainment" policy. "These concerns are rapidly coming to the view that business won by petty bribery is not desirable business anyway."[20] Business during the war was good enough to make entertaining unnecessary, but in the years ahead, most firms lost their aversion to entertaining.

"Entertainment" on an expense account often meant liquor, an essential lubricant for the wheels of commerce, particularly during the Prohibition Era. Most managers officially disapproved of its use, but sales conventions and trade meetings during the dry years often "degenerated into nothing more than drinking bouts . . . [and] one national organization spent more than $30,000 for liquor to be used in entertaining customers who attended their conventions."[21]

Entertaining was often more expensive than that. A salesman testified before the Federal Trade Commission that his company spent about 5 percent of their gross sales on showing the customers a good time. The F.T.C. ordered them to stop, but the Appeals Court reversed the ruling. Entertaining, the Court said, was as old as the hills.

Liquor was of particular concern to the sales manager who had traveling men in Europe during Prohibition. Accounts of American salesmen loose on the Continent are beyond satire. The tendency of Americans to display their patriotism when furthest from home was particularly marked among salesmen, and when combined with their cultivated enthusiasm and marinated with wine and liquor, it usually produced a rendition of "The Stars and Stripes Forever," which reverberated through the main dining room just as the other guests, from other nations, were sitting down to eat.

Entertaining was also another word for bribery. The line between the two was gray, and it faded even more when examined closely. A group of the most respectable business organizations in the country sponsored a report calling commercial bribery "a festering sore in the commercial body of the nation."[22] The only cure, they said, was major surgery. The cost of the sore was put at about $1 billion, and it proved very hard to cut out. The New York Better Business Bureau said that in New York City alone the cost was $100 million. As to how these clandestine payments were totaled is something of a mystery, but it was not true, said John T. Flynn, that "commercial bribery is . . . limited to traveling salesmen . . . and purchasing agents . . ."[23] The practice was widespread and often involved such ordinary industrial supplies as glue, dyes, and chemicals. The shipping industry was notorious for kickbacks, or Crumshaw, as payola was then called. The chainstore buyer was probably the least influenced by the temptations of the fast buck, since his buying decisions were subject to careful scrutiny.

Whatever the place of commercial bribery was, it had no place in the sales manual or in any of the theories about how goods were sold. It was a rather large omission, but an inevitable dark side of the Marketing Age.

To the manufacturer or sales manager who had struggled with the whims and demands of the buyer and the idiosyncrasies of salesmen, the Marketing Age was also the Age of Advertising. An advertising campaign had the appeal of reaching large numbers of potential customers at specified rates. Advertising was widely heralded as a valuable ally to the salesman, but it was an uneasy alliance from the beginning. The salesman saw it as competition.

The charms of advertising—or printed salesmanship, as it was called—led some managers to believe that they could dispense with the sales staff altogether and rely on direct-mail campaigns. The first copywriters, or writer-salesmen, boasted that they could "obtain equal results by the correspondence method, at lesser cost, than by the traveling salesman plan."[24]

One of the earliest sales managers to successfully combine hard selling and national advertising was Harley Procter. Procter & Gamble was a small Cincinnati soap and candle manufacturer when Procter's son Harley came into the business. He named the soap Ivory, proclaimed that it was nearly pure and that it floated. He traveled all over the country as a salesman for the firm and brought back substantial orders—seventeen carloads to one wholesaler in San Francisco. He started an advertising campaign for Ivory soap and wrote the copy himself. In 1880, he hired magazine illustrators to supply pictures for his ads. He was one of the first sales managers to think of a

national market, and one of the first users of full-page
national advertising. Procter took "an ordinary bar of
soap and made it something rather special from Maine to
California."[25]

Radio joined the national magazines in the 1920s
and added to the outpouring of appeals to buy corn
flakes, cigarettes, soap, and the whole spectrum of consumer products, thus acquainting the general public with
the realities of the age.

The year 1926 had "broken all records for general
prosperity." There was a surplus in the U. S. Treasury, and
taxes were cut by $387 million. Indeed, 1926 was "the
year of the great awakening of the nation's real resources. . . ."[26]

The Great Depression, which settled upon the nation
within three years of the great awakening, was probably
no worse on traveling men than on anyone else, but a lot
of salesmen lost their jobs, and a lot more found out that
commission on nothing was just as bad. Many sales managers refused to adjust to the realities of the Depression
and grew harsh and demanding toward their salesmen,
who accepted their lot with a sense of guilt and frustration. Had they not always believed that nothing could
stop a good salesman?

Territories were reduced to save on travel costs and
to allow for more frequent visits to customers. Hand-to-
mouth buying, which had started to replace the annual
buying trip in 1925 because of the increasingly rapid
changes in styles and merchandise, became the rule. In
1930, the hand was a little closer to the mouth. In the shoe
business, for example, the salesman who used to call on
the trade twice a year, came around once a month in
1930. The competition was fierce, and a salesman who
missed a customer when he was ready to buy lost the order to the mob.

The Depression settled the question of how the salesman would be paid and how much he should be allowed

for travel and entertainment expenses. Ninety percent of all outside salesmen were put on straight commission and had to pay their own expenses. In 1934, only 10 percent of the nearly one million salesmen received salaries, drawing accounts, or expense money.[27] Salesmen who earned a comfortable income during the twenties earned less than the NRA minimum during the thirties.*

Many traveling salesmen became agents handling more than one line, thus cutting the salesman loose from the company and bringing back an older attitude about who owned the salesman's territory. Early traveling salesmen regarded the territory and their customers as personal property. If a salesman left a company he took the customers with him. A small manufacturer employing only one salesman would have to start in business again if the salesman left.

In 1934, an affiliation of sixty-five traveling-salesman organizations petitioned President Roosevelt and testified at a hearing in Washington for a minimum wage for salesmen, but to no avail. After it was all over, a man named Arthur Marks, of Brooklyn, wrote *The New York Times* to say that the salesman had been forgotten.

* Outside salesmen were specifically excluded from all NRA codes. Samuel Untermeyer told the Traveling Salesman's Council, "You have not been overlooked. You have been deliberately, unjustly discriminated against." *The New York Times*, January 5, 1934.

Chapter Six

The Salesman
on Wheels

There were only four thousand horseless carriages built in 1900. Some of them hummed, some of them hissed, and some of them putt-putted, but none of them sounded like serious means of transportation for the professional traveler whose ear was tuned to the mighty roar of the steam locomotive.

By 1910, however, the horseless carriage had evolved into the automobile, which, as one observer correctly predicted, was pretty much like it was going to be for a while. There would be improvements made, of course, and annual style changes—a habit the car makers picked up from the bicycle industry—but the automobile was here to stay, gasoline engine and all.[1]

Production went from 180,000 in 1910 to over 1,500,-000 by 1916. In a few short years, the automobile rose, in terms of personal transportation, from almost nothing to almost everything.

The traveling man was sensitive to his means of travel. The automobile, not surprisingly, changed him quite a bit, just as it changed the whole social and economic pattern of the nation. The gift of mobility came suddenly to an eager and unsuspecting people, who asked only for more cars and more roads.

The "determination of every American to possess a motor car,"[2] as the press often reported it, was received abroad with awe and wonder. An English writer hailed popular ownership of the automobile in America as a "victory over space and time."[3] In Europe, automobiles were still considered modern chariots for the wealthy.

In order to promote the use of the automobile and encourage road building, A. L. Westgard, popular motor enthusiast of the day, left New York on October 11, 1910, on a transcontinental automobile trip. The year before, one of Mr. Ford's Model Ts had won a cross-country race to Seattle to celebrate the Alaska-Yukon-Pacific Exposition, at the blistering speed of twenty-two days. Roscoe Sheller, who later became a Ford salesman, recalled that "when the news came that [one of the cars] had crossed the Columbia River . . . and was on its way up the valley, excitement swept the community like a brush fire."[4]

The race was a sensational event that made headlines. Westgard's trip was quieter and slower and intended for the pages of *Collier's* magazine. He drove to Los Angeles in over a month and a half. His actual time was forty-one days, but he took eight days out to rest and averaged about 100 miles a day while he was on the road. His trip gave people a much better idea of what awaited the traveling public.

He took some photographs as he went, and the roads in them appeared inferior to the turnpikes built for the wagon traffic back in 1795. Roads were allowed to fall into a sad state during the railroad era. Outside of a few farm wagons, they were left to hikers until the bicycle became popular.

Westgard found that the road between Columbus and Indianapolis had a mound of gravel running down the center where work crews had dumped it. Cars were forced to drive with one wheel off the road, usually in a ditch, giving the passenger a bumpy and angular ride for some miles. Crossing Iowa, however, he found excellent roads, maintained by the farmers, who dragged and scraped them on a set day.

In New Mexico, his trip was slowed by deep sand, packs of coyotes, and a scarcity of gasoline. Other travelers reported that western roads generally were quite treacherous, and while trips to Florida required bravery, to venture into Texas, one needed "unparalleled heroism." Even in the South, roads were passable to the "ordinary automobile," although one was urged to take caution "off the beaten path," a description that was no idle cliché.[5]

While auto touring in the countryside was depicted as adventurous or uplifting, the cities were already experiencing traffic jams in 1910. The year before, the editor of *Horseless Age* had predicted that the use of automobiles would relieve traffic jams. The magazine had a history of being wrong. The editor in 1896 had predicted the auto would reduce the accident rate because the machine would not shy and run away. A description of those "long unending jams" has a distinctly modern ring: "They fill the air with the strong odor of gasolene [sic] and emit choking, coughing sounds." Beauty was often in the ear of the beholder. To the man breezing down the country road, "the engine sang sweet and true. The exhaust sounded full and snappy."[6]

By 1920, traffic jams were common features in even the small towns on Sunday afternoon, when everyone in the whole country who had a car went out for a drive. Everyone, that is, except the traveling man, and that was his day off.

The automobile was consuming gas at such a rate that, by 1925, it was thought that a new unit of liquid measure would have to be found, since the gallon was such an insignificant part of the six and a quarter billion gallons being gulped annually. Automobile statistics were as big a rage as the automobile, and popular magazines never seemed to tire of printing new ones—sixty-two million feet of brake lining was used in 1924, enough to reach halfway round the world, and it would have taken two hundred fully loaded freight cars to carry the iron used in the license plates.

No one ever totaled the number or value of barnyard animals that fell victim to the automotive invasion of the countryside, but a poem that appeared in 1911 noted that only prize chickens of great value were allowed to wander untended about the country roads:

> . . . skidding wheel and jarring shock
> Proclaimed thou wert a Plymouth Rock.
> Alas! I know not where or when
> I've run across so dear a hen.[7]

The automobile itself was at first a subject for humor. George Ade called it a movable madhouse, and there were enough jokes about the Ford to print a whole book of them. But for the traveling man, the automobile was a serious matter. A 1920 survey of 10,000 car owners showed that only one car in ten was purely for recreation. Traveling salesmen, according to the survey, "doubled, tripled, and in some cases, quadrupled their business through the use of their cars."[8] Farmers, who in popular humor taunted city slickers with such gems as "get a horse," were found to be heavy users of the auto, and in many ways were more dependent on the car than anyone else.

The traveling man was such a good customer of the new industry that in 1922 one manufacturer made a car especially for salesmen. It had the rugged durability of a truck and could take the salesman to the muddiest, remotest corner of his territory. It had the style and trim of a car, and there was plenty of storage room behind the driver's seat. The trunk opened up to reveal a chest of drawers suitable for a sample display.

The Bureau of Labor Statistics made its first survey of automobile usage in 1936 and found that the traveling salesman was the nation's leading driver. The average traveling man put 18,791 miles a year on his car, as compared to a little over 8000 for the national average.

The automobile had a great influence on the size of a salesman's territory and the manner in which he covered it. Territories that in the past were divided geographically were now divided into car territories and train territories. The salesman, by car, was usually able to see more of his customers more often, particularly in the small towns. In many cases, a company was able to use fewer salesmen to bring in more business, a trend that was offset by the current vogue of smaller territories and bigger quotas. The nation's economy was rapidly expanding, and each year the salesman was expected to bring in more business from his territory, and in almost every case the salesman with a car did.

Printer's Ink reported that every sales manager they queried said it cost about 15 percent more to send out traveling salesmen in automobiles than by train.[9] In spite of the increase in sales, a lot of grumbling was heard about the cost of keeping the salesman on wheels. It was hard for some business managers to keep in mind that the crucial figure was the cost of the car as compared to sales, not as compared to trains. "Too many companies," said *Sales Management,* "are overlooking the fact that they are employing salesmen to make sales at a profit—not to operate automobiles at a savings."[10]

If a salesman hustled around his territory and increased his sales by a third, many companies were apt to grumble that he wore out a new set of tires. If he hit two towns a day instead of one, as he did on the train, the company was likely to note only that he forgot to put oil in the car and burned out a bearing.

The cost of the salesman's car and who should own it were the burning issues in the business press during the 1920s. It was the consensus that it was cheaper if the salesman drove a company car, and it was also more likely that he would drive it on rutted, washboard roads if the car wasn't his. Companies with rural territories preferred to provide the salesman with a car. Pride of ownership was considered one of the advantages of having the salesman own his car, provided he was not so protective of it that he would drive it only in fair weather and on good roads.

Record-keeping was greatly simplified when it came to compensating the salesman for the use of his own car. He was paid a mileage allowance, and that was the end of it, although some companies retained a portion of the allowance against the day he would have to buy a new car.

Record-keeping and cost control were not so simple for companies who maintained sizable fleets of cars. Standard Oil had over 1700 cars for its sales and service department, Associated Bell Telephone had over 1200, and Armour & Co. and Shell of California had more than 1000 each. Procter & Gamble had 450 cars at the disposal of their salesmen, and in 1927 they had operating costs down to a little less than a nickel a mile.

Fords were the cheapest cars to operate, but one manufacturer said that salesmen generally neglected them, "but take a personal pride in other cars."

The shortage of salesmen during the First World War hastened the use of the automobile to allow fewer men to cover larger territories. In some parts of the country, neither the train nor the car alone was quite what the salesman needed. For the salesman with a big territory, it was better to take the train between cities and use a car at each stop. In New England, where the distances between customers was not great, a salesman could cover his territory easily in his own car. But

in the larger states, like Ohio and in the South and the
West, the salesman had a special need. He either had to
own a car in each city or he had to be able to rent somebody else's. A traveling man who owned a car and shared
it, for a fee, with another salesman, found that not only
did he have to pay higher insurance rates, but that two
salesmen in the same car led to trouble. If he was selling
and his passenger was waiting, he felt he had to rush. If
his passenger was selling and he was waiting, he fumed.
In neither case did a passenger help his sales effort, and
the fee wasn't worth the aggravation.

The first car-rental agency was the Ford Livery
Company of Omaha.[11] It started one winter afternoon in
1915 in a real estate and loan office. One of the men in the
office borrowed a car for the second time that day and
suggested to the owner that they should find some basis
of paying for the use of the car. It occurred to the owner
that if one person were willing to rent his car, there
might be others. Next year, he offered new cars for ten
cents a mile, gasoline and oil extra, and a minimum
charge of fifty cents an hour. "Just like the old-time livery
barn," said the first ad, "only we rent you a new 1917
Ford Motor Car instead of a horse and buggy." By 1925,
car-rental services were available in most towns and cities
of any size.

Morris and Company, a Chicago packer, was an early
user of rented cars. Their salesmen in the Northwest used
hired cars to work the small towns. According to Dartnell, "The results were astounding, both from the stand-
point of increased orders and a marked increase in good
spirits and enthusiasm on the part of the salesmen themselves."[12]

Before long, it was discovered that salesmen with
cars covered the territory too well, and had time left
over. The territories were soon expanded, and fewer
salesmen were employed to bring in the same volume of
business.

In the Southwest, Morris used forty-five salesmen to cover the territory by train. The men were constantly on the move, and many small towns were skipped altogether. When these men were given cars, they covered every crossroads store and still had time left over. The selling force of forty-five men was reduced to nine men, and business increased.

The same was true in Oregon and parts of Washington and Idaho, where "The Northeast oleomargarine trade was covered by one man in a car, whereas it used to take five men to cover this same territory by rail."[13]

Many travelers with big territories still preferred to drive the whole way, particularly in summer, when the sleeper on the train was like an oven. Quite often, by the time a salesman had waited for his train and changed at the next station for another train, he arrived at his destination in the small hours. By car, a drive of four or five hours was preferred if he could arrive in time for dinner and forego the physical work of moving his sample trunks out of trains and in and out of hotels. They stayed tucked away in the back of his car until it was time to show them to the buyer. Of course, his car and his samples might be stolen, as some 35,000 car thefts took place in 1922.

Before the salesman took to the car, every village with a population of over 1500 had a "drummer joint," usually called the Grand Hotel, across from the train station. It featured lumpy food and mattresses and catered largely to the traveling man trapped between trains. With the appearance of the auto, they got what most of them deserved. The salesman drove on past, and they very quickly lost business to the new "motels" or drastically improved. In fact, salesmen were so intent on making the next city with decent hotels and restaurants that they developed what became known as hit-and-run selling. The salesman who traveled by train had a certain leisurely pace forced on him by the railroad timetable. But now the salesman couldn't get through his territory fast enough. Some even went so far as to leave their cars parked in front of the merchant's store with the motor running. The merchant, seeing the salesman in such a hurry, would tell him, "See me next time." Next time, like tomorrow, never comes. One salesman reflected on how he and most of the other salesmen never seemed to have time any more. They used to spend some time with the dealers and help them trim their windows—the salesman would see that he put his own product up front —and talk with the dealer about his problems. He gave up his car and went back to traveling on the train and found that his sales volume increased by 27 percent. He was, ironically, a salesman of auto parts.

Though mass-produced, many of the first automobiles had individual temperaments when it came to starting in the morning and handling on the road. They were not immediately welcomed by many traveling salesmen who had been accustomed to the pleasures of first-class train travel at a time when the best restaurants in America were on the railroads. The man who left the train for the car was often disenchanted. Richardson Haw, a traveling salesman for the Richmond Guano Company, learned how to drive a Model T and immediately set out to call on his customers. By the time he got to Raleigh he was so exasperated with the damn thing that when the bell captain asked him if he wanted his car parked, Haw replied, "Park my car? You may have it. I never want to see it again."*

Nevertheless, most salesmen were sold on the automobile, and advertisements for traveling salesmen used a fancy car as an inducement. The kind of car, it was realized, would indicate a great deal about the status of the salesman and his company. A Ford was fine for calling on the grocery trade, but a salesman calling on busi-

* His daughter told me this story.

nessmen should drive a Paige, or even a Marmon. "Some salesmen feel that on account of the fun that is made of Fords they do not like to call on the trade in one."[14] Nevertheless, Standard Oil, Colgate, Armour, and the Peet Brothers sent their men out in Fords. Pittsburgh Plate Glass, American Can, and Toledo Scale preferred the Overland cars. Goodyear, Western Electric, and American Tobacco used the Saxon.

There was always some dispute over allowing for the salesman's private use of the car. The Sperry Flour Company of Seattle tried to discourage the salesmen by painting the cars white, with a big Sperry trademark on the door. Most companies' names were put on the door for advertising as well. Occasionally a merchant would give an order to a salesman of a product he'd been meaning to try because he just happened to see the fellow's car parked out on the street. The Chicago Trust Company refrained from advertising itself on the bank's cars, since their representatives were often out arranging real estate loans, and the customer might not want the whole neighborhood to know he was borrowing money.

The other common feature of the company car was a governor, set at about forty miles an hour, since the traveling man—in the company's view—was a real rakehell behind the wheel.

The salesman was always under suspicion of using the car to pad his expense account. W. K. Kellogg, the manufacturer of corn flakes, was crossing the country by train when somewhere in the middle of the Iowa night he looked out the window and saw a Kellogg company automobile parked on the street. At the next stop he sent a telegram back to Battle Creek to find out if the salesman in that territory had charged up garage rent on his expense account.[15]

Most sales managers were reluctant to "hammer down" on the salesman about the cost of operating his car. They were afraid they might spoil his disposition.

As the 1920s closed with the Great Depression, such gentle considerations were all but forgotten. Mileage allowances were cut back in some companies to as little as four cents a mile, and a few companies paid only for the number of miles between towns, a figure they arrived at themselves by consulting the map. This ignored the actual mileage incurred in detours and multiple stops in the same town.

Territories were greatly reduced during the Depression because buyers were more conservative and bought in smaller lots, though more frequently.

The Depression marked an end to many things, and one of them was the business debut of the automobile. It was commonplace and accepted by then, and like many things with which we become familiar, it was subsequently ignored, at least by traveling men.

Today, it has been estimated that 80 percent of all salesmen travel primarily by automobile. The car will probably be air conditioned and will not be a compact. "This is the salesman's office," said one car-fleet executive. "They want him to be happy in it."[16]

Chapter Seven

The Sensible, Logical Engineer

The clock, the cash register, and the automobile were among the products that America gave to the world in quantity, thus reflecting in the development of mass production our preoccupations with time, money, and mobility.

The demands of faster and cheaper production called for machines of increasing complexity and variety, and a need soon developed for industrial salesmen who not only could comprehend the technology, but who could apply it to new uses. These salesmen did not call on the general public or the retailer, but found their trade among the production managers, plant superintendents, and others involved in the manufacturing process.

Charles M. Schwab, president of the Carnegie Steel Company, was one of the first big employers of technical-school graduates as salesmen. He put them in the blooming mills and blast furnaces, and before the open hearth for two years before they began their sales training. Selling, in his opinion, did not depend on a lot of flowery talk. The customer was a technical man—sensible and logical—and so must the salesman be.

The image of the sales engineer was in sharp contrast to the prevailing ideas about salesmen. Beginning in about 1900, one found many comparisons between the old-time salesman full of hot air and the new engineer salesman sworn to logic. The technical salesman was accorded something of a professional standing, although at first there was some confusion over which salesmen would be accorded this new status. The distinction was made between the salesmen who sold staples and those who sold specialties. The man who sold staples was the "typical drummer." The specialty salesman was a "specialist" in either one article or line of goods, such as "an adding machine, a vacuum cleaner, or a restricted line of supplies or tools used in manufacturing. His samples may consist of a few well-arranged facts, backed by a few photographs. The drummer is old, the specialty salesman is new."[1] New, of course, was better.

The vacuum cleaner was soon dropped from the specialty list as it became common. Then, too, it was sold directly to the consumer, and there never had been much status attached to selling to *people*, coming, as it does, so close to peddling. The salesman, careful of his image, preferred to call on *buyers*. The sales engineer, as the "specialist" came to be called, preferred not to think of himself as a salesman at all. "Certainly the work of the sales engineer requires the application of the scientific method and rational processes. Only in this way can one engineer persuade and help another engineer, and that is what is involved in the sales engineer's work."[2]

If there was some worry among engineers that selling was not a proper occupation for a professional man, he was assured that in the technical world fast developing, he was—as a salesman—the man of the hour.

Two surveys made in 1939 showed that the engineering student was actually more inclined to sales work than the commercial or liberal arts student, the majority of whom regarded selling as "an undesirable racket or as work for morons."[3] The engineering students worried more about the insecurity of commissions, apparently unaware that most sales engineers were paid a straight salary.

The term "sales engineer" originally referred to engineers who were assigned to the sales department to demonstrate new products to prospective customers or to function as trouble shooters. Gilbert Rigg, a sales engineer for the New Jersey Zinc Company from 1911 to 1916, said that he "never sold one pennyworth of anything in my life as a sales engineer. It is not part of my job. A sales engineer is not a salesman."[4]

It was not until the Depression that the sales engineer was generally recognized as a salesman of industrial products. This evolution came about as the result of a number of historic events.

The marketing problems attendant on overproduction did not hit the industrial producer at the same time or in the same way as it did the manufacturer of consumer products. The industrial producers who made the machines—and ancillary products—that made mass production possible, concerned themselves very little with sales. The buyer of technical goods and supplies was forced to rely on independent consulting engineers to help him with his purchases if he lacked the expertise. The industrial manufacturers were of little help in providing reliable information or assistance. Not until the Depression did the problems of distribution seem as important as "invention, design, and production."[5]

The Depression, which increased the demand for sales engineers, also provided a manpower pool of technical-school graduates who were unable to find employment. Large numbers of new engineers and budding scientists became salesmen.[6]

Throughout most of history, productivity has decreased in wartime. But the Industrial Revolution made war dependent on production. The British said that the factory chimneys of Manchester were the guns that won the battle of Waterloo.[7] In the wars of this century, more men went to work in the factories than went to fight in the trenches. Wars, instead of reducing productive capacity, now increase it.

The Second World War changed the nature of production in a profound and basic way. Instead of buying only raw materials, manufacturers often bought finished components. "The completely integrated producer, who manufactured everything that was required for his production, disappeared from the American scene. . . . With the existence of two primary classes of industrial producers, the assembler and the component producer, it became evident that a sustaining marketing link would have to be established . . ."[8] This link was supplied by the sales engineer.

Jack Rashba was among the first wave of sales engineers. He graduated from Yale in 1923 with a Master's Degree in Electrical Engineering. He went to work for the New Haven Railroad as an assistant engineer in the testing department, where he was mainly involved in evaluating products that the buyers for the railroad were not qualified to judge. Manufacturers were able to rig tests that favored their products, and in the absence of reliable or comprehensible information, the decision to buy was occasionally made over a few drinks and money under the table.

Rashba dealt with all kinds of companies. "I represented a big railroad. All these outfits were intensely interested in getting a position, so that I was an important individual to them. And of course, I got the glad hand, which was my first introduction to a phase of selling I had to get pretty deep into later on myself."

In one Chicago plant he inspected a performance test on a turbine the railroad was interested in. "They put a load on the electrical end, and then they would measure the amount of steam that was used." The less the water that was collected, the more efficient the turbine. "Previously on this test maybe the chief clerk would come and stand by and they'd run the test and give him the results and that would be it. I noticed there was a little angle offshoot at the bottom and some of the steam was being carried off. I didn't say anything until the test was over and they were getting the results. I said, 'What do you imagine the weight was of the water that went by this little bypass.' Well, that really ran into consternation." After profuse exclaiming about whether such a thing could happen, Rashba was asked to stay over for another test the next morning. "I was introduced to the Loop that night and really sent on the town, with pressed duck and all. So I got various facets of what was involved in a product and in selling and promoting. It was invaluable."

The New Haven, being an electrified railroad, bought a lot of high-voltage cable. To qualify for purchase, it had to be tested for 10,000 volts for five minutes. "Now, the average materials inspector they had at the time could count the number of straws in a broom, but he had no electrical background, and anyone could readily put a six-volt buzzer somewhere in the room and tell him that was 10,000 volts."

One of the items that was in steady demand was asbestos-covered wire supplied by the Rockbestos Company. The test for the wire "usually got to four minutes and forty-five seconds, and then whamo." Rashba made some suggestions about the manufacture of the wire that helped the company get past the test as well as improve the wire.

After he had been with the New Haven about two years, the president of Rockbestos offered him a job. Rashba had already decided that there was no great future for him with the railroad. The job he was offered involved a good deal of travel and paid more money.

In 1925, Rashba became a sales engineer, but at first he was to be more engineer than salesman. He traveled all over the country, calling on railroads, coal mines, and steel mills, demonstrating, and looking for, new uses for asbestos-covered wire. In many of the plants he visited no one had ever heard of Rockbestos. Company salesmen were often afraid to call on industrial users because "someone might ask them a question about the dielectric breakdown characteristics or what have you." In the coal mines, he found a great need for a cable that was both waterproof and fireproof. He returned to the company and worked with the production department in developing a cable insulation combining varnished cambric sandwiched between walls of felted asbestos, denoted as AVC cable. AVC soon became an industry standard and Rockbestos patented it, although they eventually licensed other companies to make it rather than defend the patent in court.

In 1927, Rashba became a full-time salesman, with Pennsylvania, Ohio, and the South as his territory. Asbestos-insulated cable was a new concept at that time and considerably more costly than conventional available cable. It was essential to determine the proper applications that would justify the increased cost.

Until 1933, he was a bachelor, and while he covered his territory by train, streetcar, and on foot—taking great pride in his thrift by avoiding rented cars and taxicabs— he did enjoy the pleasures of the Read House in Chattanooga and the famous Maxwell House in Nashville. "In the years between 1927 and 1933, I really didn't mind being away. Wherever I hung my pajamas was home. On the southern trips I usually stayed two weeks. I'd wind up in

Cincinnati at the end of the week and then go down and spend the weekend in Birmingham and the following week in Atlanta and Tennessee."

Sometime in the early thirties, the Ohio territory was taken away from him and set up as a separate territory. "Frankly, I had developed the Ohio area, the hard way with my coattails out. If I do say, without much of a to-do, they simply told me that they were going to open up an office in Cleveland. In the forties, they opened up an office to take care of the southern territory, and about that time I'd had it as far as really chasing around was concerned." (He was married then.)

In spite of the emphasis on technical knowledge, all of his selling was not cut and dried. He recalled one instance with an electrical engineer of a steel mill he had been trying to sell for a couple of years. "That fellow was an absolute czar. I'd call and send in my card, talk to the boys, but he was always busy. One time I came there and he happened to be free. I talked to him a little bit about wire, then he had a phone call. His broker called him about some Studebaker stock and I made some comment on the market, enough so that it was obvious to him that I wasn't just reading a headline, you know. I was able to draw on my experiences and I sat there for forty-five minutes with him. Then he says to me, 'I'm going down to the shop. Would you like to come down and meet our chief maintenance man?' When he introduced me, that was almost a command." Rashba had many similar experiences over the years. "Selling wasn't just knowing your product."

Jack Rashba retired in 1968. He spent over forty years as a traveling man in wire and cable. He was glad to be out of the business, which had changed too much for his taste. "I always had a cigar to hand out. Outside of a few lunches, I didn't find it necessary to go into entertaining on the scale they do today. The electrical end of things was a great unknown in those days. Most of the people I called on were glad to see me and hear my views.

"There isn't much room for individuality at these big companies, and there's no opportunity for the salesman to show his entrepreneurial ability." Technology, too, has changed. "Modern electronic development passes me by."

"However, in retrospect, the years spent with Rockbestos as a sales engineer and finally as District Sales Manager had rich rewards in the number of cherished friends that I made with a variety of people from top management down the line. My dealings through the years with management were mutually friendly. The president gave me a beautiful retirement party graced by company officials and wives. Some hundred business associates and wives had been invited."

In spite of the wide influence John Patterson had on salesmanship, Rashba had never heard of him. He never received any sales training, he never had any quota but "Do the best you can," he never had to sing any company songs or take part in any sales contests. His sales manager never gave him any pep talks, and no one ever attempted to improve upon his native enthusiasm.

Many sales engineers who began their careers in the twenties, as Jack Rashba did, became manufacturers' agents, or independent sales agents—which amounted to the same thing—during the Depression. There were about 10,000 reps and agents in 1939, and the number doubled in the early forties.

The agent found a special place in industry as the trend toward the component-assembler relationship developed. Many small companies were unable to support a sales staff large enough to give them adequate market coverage. By using agents, a small component maker could, in effect, gain wide distribution without the risk of high sales expenses that might yield few sales. The independent agent worked a familiar territory and carried a compatible line of goods. He worked on straight commission and paid his own expenses.

The ideal agent specialized in a relatively narrow range. Rashba, for example, might have become a sales agent for other types of electrical insulated cables. He could have represented a number of manufacturers. Each company that gave him a line to rep would have gained an experienced salesman with a well-developed territory, cultivated over many years and containing many buyers who were accessible to Rashba. The same companies, if they hired their own salesman, might have got a less-experienced man who had less product knowledge, and was less well-known to the trade. During the time it took the new salesman to establish himself, his salary would have been a loss to the company and he might produce few sales.

Even a large company might contract a sales agent to handle a new product or a special product that was dissimilar to their main line.

Many companies used sales agents to introduce a product into the market, and once sales were established, they would hire a salesman—for less than the agent's commission. This was—and is—a source of frustration to the agent. After he had spent years establishing a product in his territory, he often saw it taken away and given to a company salesman just as it was beginning to bring in commissions.

For many years the number of agents and representatives increased, but the trend now seems to be moving to the hired sales force, particularly in specialized industries such as electronics. Product lines are becoming more complex, and to an increasing degree products are tailored to specialized needs. An agent with eight or nine different lines finds it increasingly difficult to keep up with technological advances.

The advantages of hiring a salesman or contracting an agent may be debated endlessly. The wise choice depended on the needs of the moment.

The engineer as salesman—whether agent or hired—

had one failing. He was taught that "the industrial sale
is always made on the basis of cold, hard facts, con-
cretely proven by test, research, experiment, and experience . . ."⁹ Those cold, hard facts quite often pre-
vented the sales engineer from coming to grips with the
warm, soft soul of the buyer. The sales engineer had a
tendency to lecture, to become bogged down in the product specifications, while ignoring the real needs of his
customer. He took offense if his facts were doubted, and
was easily drawn into a heated argument if they were
disputed. Feeling himself the authority on his product, he
had difficulty understanding why the buyer did not buy,
once its obvious superiority had been explained. The sales
engineer thus rebuffed, responded with more facts and
figures instead of responding as a salesman would—back
off and look for the real objection.

The picture of the overly technical salesman which I
have presented is a stereotype, no more or less accurate
than the image of the nontechnical salesman who wore
loud clothes and told dirty jokes. All stereotypes bear a
grain of truth, and enough sales engineers were beating
their customers over the head with their slide rules to
cause concern on the part of management. It was realized
that to get a sales engineer you could take an engineer
and make him a salesman, or you could take a salesman
and teach him some engineering.

There was a growing recognition that in all selling
there is some personality. Some influence is exerted that
cannot be weighed, measured, titrated, assigned a log-
arithm, or viewed under a microscope. Within the breast
of every sensible, logical engineer who wants to sell, must
beat a salesman's heart.

After World War II, American industry began in
earnest to recruit engineers for the sales department and
to provide extensive technical training to nonengineers.
It was no longer a matter of having some engineers
around to say a few words in technicalese to impress the

customers. Nor was it enough to employ engineers to explain what the company had to sell. The sales engineer was forced into a more aggressive salesmanship, which meant making his quota, singing a few company songs, and competing in sales contests.

The specter of overproduction which had haunted the 1920s had been held at bay by a depression and a war. In 1946, a marketing executive wrote that Americans would have to live 50 percent better in the future—that is, they would have to consume more goods. "Whatever the increased percentage of national consumption that may actually be achieved, no one will object to proposition. Actually, there appears to be no choice in the matter. Having the production potentials which are so high . . . that they strain the imagination, we turn instinctively to the only possible answer to the impending 'Niagara' of production. . . . The answer is *selling, selling,* and more *selling*."[10]

Chapter Eight

The On-line, Real Time, Traveling Computer Salesman

There evolved from the sales engineer a real live salesman, fully trained but fully a salesman. He had regained some of the lost stature of the salesmen of earlier days, and lost none of his dignity for it. The most prestigious salesmen on the road in the last decade were from the electronics industry. The degree to which these men tended to be *traveling* salesmen varied with the company they worked for, the type of product they sold, and the industry they covered.

A salesman for electronic data-processing equipment for general business use often found his territory confined to a few city blocks or even to a few floors of a single building. Within this relatively small area, he found all the customers he could handle. A salesman of scientific computers, however, was likely to have a much bigger territory simply because there were fewer users of this type of computer. He had to have a big territory to have enough customers.

Jerome T. Paul was a computer salesman who started out in one of those dense urban territories, and eventually serviced a territory bound only by the continental limits of the United States. From covering Long Island City on foot, he graduated to covering the country by jet.

His story is illustrative of how the traveling man operates today on the most sophisticated level. In many ways, Jerry resembles the traveling men of the past. In the tradition of the peddler, he looked to a territory to escape from the lack of opportunity in his neighborhood. And in the tradition of the drummer, he has an old-fashioned, oversized ego and an appetite for first-class living. He is alert and full of the necessary intelligence and aggressiveness. He is both charming and abrasive.

Jerry was born in New York City, attended public schools and high school in Queens. His family was "relatively poor," and Jerry—metaphorically and, to an extent, literally—grew up in the street. At school, Jerry did well in math and was advised to become an accountant, a piece of advice that recognized a facility but ignored his basic character.

He went to City College at night, and prepared himself to be a CPA. He was in a hurry, although he wasn't yet sure where he was hurrying. He managed to graduate in four years by holding down a full-time job during the day and taking a heavy course load at night, four years of summer school, and, once, a class on his lunch hour.

For the first three years at college he worked as a clerk and became increasingly convinced that he was never going to be an accountant. In his last year at college he took a job with the Round Tire and Rubber Company as a retail tire salesman. "Sheer money. I made no long-

range career goals. I fundamentally believed there was
more money in selling."

The first product Jerry sold was a very expensive
tire. In 1955, it sold for $100. "It took a little romance to
sell that." If a customer seemed ripe, he would be shown
a ten-minute movie full of the tragedies of driving on anything but Round Tire's hundred-dollar beauties. His biggest personal triumph in selling came when he sold five
of them to a Dale Dance Studio instructor with a four-
year-old car.

After six months of handling the off-the-street trade,
he spent a year in the commercial tire division and began
to get some of the hard-nosed experience that became the
rock foundation of his knowledge about selling, even
though it was the rock bottom of his career in other ways.
Jerry was transferred to the Bronx office, which turned out
to be a large overhead garage full of tires, telephones, and
filing cabinets. His main task was calling on bald-tire
prospects. "You walk around looking for trucks with bald
tires. When you find one you check the card file back in
the office and make sure none of the other salesmen have
the account. Then you make a cold call on the company
that owned the truck and try to sell a set of tires or re-
tread of the bald tires."

The companies that used significant numbers of
truck tires in the Bronx were filled with some tough customers. "What it does, calling on that crud and dealing
with those people, it makes you very hard and insensitive
to abuse. I remember one time I called on a bald-tire
prospect at the Pile Rug Cleaning Company. Guy's name
was Oldmun. I stumbled through the warehouse where
his office was and said 'Hi, I'm your friendly Round Tire
and Rubber salesman,' to which he replied 'You *******,
get your ******* out of my office before I throw your
******* down those ******* stairs, and break every
bone in your ******* body.'

"I said, 'Gee, sir, you must have had some small

trouble with our product in the past.' And he told me how a tire blew out and almost killed his whole family. But that kind of reception wasn't unusual. The other problem was that a lot of buyers were on the take.

"A garage manager might say 'Sure, gimme a set of whitewalls for my car and we can do some business.' Of course, his company would pay for them without knowing it. If it violated your principles, you shouldn't be there. It was one of the reasons I didn't like the tire business, but that's the way it was. In many ways it was a very dirty business, and it wasn't long before I realized that it wasn't what I wanted to do. Nobody was getting rich at it. The sales manager made around $18,000 plus an expense account that allowed him to drink like a fish, and a good salesman who had been there a long time made between $14,000 and $16,000. In the short time I was there I made $700 to $1000 a month. It was better than the $70 a week I was getting as a clerk at UPI after three years. By this time, I had graduated from college, I was married and I knew I wanted to be a salesman. I got a smell of IBM and applied for a job. When I approached the company I was dressed in their image. I adopted as much of the Ivy League styles as I could—accent and mannerisms—because IBM was classically a rich boys' haven. I wore a hat because IBM salesmen always wear hats. Actually, I wore a hat at Round Tire, but I made sure I wore it to call on IBM.

"I was interviewed by the branch manager, and I was impressed because he was young to be in management. He was thirty-six or thirty-seven. In my own experience at UPI no one got into management unless they had been there twenty-three years and had been a writer before that. Round Tire wasn't much different, except that it helped to be Irish Catholic.

"In the course of the conversation he let me know that he owned a Jaguar and lived in Port Washington

and only came into this depressed neighborhood because that's where his branch was.

"The offices were all carpeted and the secretaries
were well-groomed and one could see that whoever
joined that illustrative team was well-rewarded.

"It was my good fortune to always test well. I had
taken courses in industrial psychology and I knew how
the tests were structured and I could often tell what they
were looking for. In their hearts they were looking for
someone who was creative and had guts. Unfortunately,
in their tests they were looking for the most stable, mid-
dle-of-the-road, professional types they could find. I did
well in the tests and they were thrilled with me in the
Bronx office of IBM. I was about to accept a job when I
got my draft notice. I spent two years, less a few months.
I got out early for being a chimney sweep. If you had a
seasonal occupation the Army would let you out if you
had a job offer. All you needed was a letter."

After getting his discharge, Jerry looked around for
a position with a half-dozen companies, but he still
thought about that job at IBM. He had heard the stories
about new salesmen making $25,000 to $35,000 a year. It
sounded good. His apprenticeship at Round Tire was
over, and with a new baby in the house, Jerry was ready
to make some money.

He returned to the Bronx office of IBM at his cocky
best and left a little nervous. They had no "head count,"
i.e., they weren't hiring, but because he had done so well
on those tests, he was directed to the Manhattan branch
office on Church Street.

"Now *this* was a branch office. You really had the
feeling of a colossal dark-suited, white-shirted, hatted
world of efficient, bright, Ivy League people in the computer business, making it whirl and think. After I was interviewed, they asked me what I needed, minimum, and
I think I sweated out $450 a month. They made it $475,
and boy, was I impressed. Looking back, I think I was

asking for less than the minimum. I even might have gotten $650."

For the next fifteen months, Jerry went through various training schools. He learned to wire unit-record (punchcard) equipment and program computers. He went to applications school and sales school.

In his first school, where he learned to operate and install unit-record machines, the class standing was recorded and posted every week. Out of a class of twenty-one, he was eleventh. His branch manager called him into his office and told him that, according to his class standing, he was exactly in the middle. He was the best of the worst, and the worst of the best, and he'd better move his ass.

Jerry soon discovered that competition for a good territory had already begun. He settled down and improved his standing to a respectable sixth before the class was over.

Following the school, there were a few months of on-the-job training—"wiring boards" to make the little holes in the punch cards do the right things. Two months of programming school came next, and then a stint back at the branch helping a senior salesman in his territory, calling on customers and writing proposals.

This time he was on his own, because the salesman who owned the territory had an account *on status*. The customer was paying, say, $5000 a month and getting about $2000 a month worth of service out of his computer, and he was, understandably, screaming, "Get that goddamn thing out of here, *now*." The salesman, in such circumstances, works full time trying to keep the machine in, and files frequent "status reports" (a pink copy goes to the branch office, a green copy goes to the regional office, a yellow copy goes to headquarters, etc.). Company executives flock around to assist by looking over his shoulder and wringing their hands. The only thing worse than having an account on status is to have a machine

thrown out without having ever been on status. Such a
lack of account control may well cost a salesman his job,
or at least land him in a remote territory similar to that
given to a cop who tickets the Mayor's car.

Jerry was a sales trainee for fifteen months. The
average time was eighteen months to two years. Some
salesmen had been trainees for as long as four years when
there had been a shortage of systems engineers and many
trainees were put to work installing new equipment. A
more usual reason for a long tenure as trainee was being
outpaced by one's peers. When a territory becomes available, it goes to the man who did the best in school and
had the best sales-training record. The best go fastest.
Even the time the trainee goes to his second training
school is determined by his previous record. *Everything* is
an indication of how the fledgling salesman is progressing.
And if you're not progressing too well the indications are
daily humiliations. Those who play through have about
them the aura of promise. They are further assisted by
the branch manager, upon whom the trainee's rapid
progress is a warm reflection.

In spite of the long training period in those days,
the average salesman remained in a territory, and on
quota, for only eighteen months before he was promoted
or reassigned to a nonquota job, because the company
was growing so rapidly. IBM is a sales-oriented company, and the division, group, and corporate offices are
dominated by former salesmen. The brief stint in the
territory determines to a large extent the future success
of the man in the company. Having a good territory—
earned by being an outstanding trainee—is the equivalent
of going to a good school, and a good sales record is like
graduating with honors.

In one common path of ascension, a good salesman
was sent to Endicott or Poughkeepsie for two years to
teach applications school and sales school, and then he
became an assistant branch manager, thus beginning his

rise toward the corporate godhead. Back then, if you weren't a salesman, you weren't going anywhere.

At applications school, trainees were taught cost accounting, payroll systems, and business methods. Jerry sailed through the five-week course, made the second highest grades in his class, and was awarded a pair of gold cufflinks. His closest rival from the Church Street branch was Roger Smith. Roger had gone to Princeton, said he crewed on Mr. Watson's yacht, and had been a bright star as a trainee. Jerry estimated that, on the basis of the number of people who claimed to have crewed on Mr. Watson's yacht, it was a vessel some 3000 feet long which sailed eight days a week. He later discovered an even more amazing fact. Based on the number of people he met who claimed to live "next to Tom," he estimated that Mr. Watson lived in Greenwich on a star-shaped piece of property slightly larger than the state of Connecticut.

Roger had been first man in his class at the technical school for unit-record equipment and had done well in the field. He had been sent to applications school two weeks ahead of Jerry, a significant indication of his prowess. But now the tide was turning in Jerry's favor. He returned to the branch a hero. Roger had finished sixth or seventh in his class and was very upset about it.

Back at the branch office he was filling in for a senior salesman who had some equipment on status. IBM had just announced a small scientific computer, and Jerry had demonstrated it to a customer who was very interested. He spent a week on the sale and came away with the first order for the new computer. He followed this triumph with a sale to a scientific supply house that was one of the biggest orders they ever had for a new customer in the branch. It earned a $10,000 commission for the salesman who owned the territory, but Jerry, though no richer in money, was now the undisputed comer. His sales as a trainee were credited to the salesman who held the territory. He put two salesmen in the 100 percent Club by his efforts.

Shortly afterward, Jerry was off to sales school, and again he returned to the branch with a pair of gold cufflinks and miles ahead of old Roger.

"Sold three new accounts and, boy, I was hot as a pistol. I was so hot other sales trainees who were about my vintage or a few months behind me would sit down and say, 'How are you doing it, Paul?' It was strange. I was embarrassed. I was lucky, timing was good, I was rather bright and not a bad peddler and working hard, and I had a nose for where the action was, and I'd go chase the action.

"Before I leave sales school they tell me I have been selected for a nice lush fat territory. There are 66,222 installed points* in it. That was pretty big bananas in those days. It was comprised of twenty-eight fire and casualty insurance companies as customers."

His prospecting territory was between Fourteenth and Fortieth streets and the north side of Maiden Lane. "Day I get back I get in at 7:30 in the morning, rush to my desk to get it all cleaned up. There were one or two people in there and they're uneasy as hell. There's a big note on my desk: 'Speak to D.P. first thing this morning.' I go in—big comfortable office—and he says, 'Jerry, I don't know how to tell you this. The territory we gave you isn't yours any more.'

"I was stunned. I was really stunned. He said, 'Well, a desperate situation came and we needed a man of your caliber. Out in Queens.'

"'I don't want to go to Queens. I like it here, sir. What reward is that for outstanding work?' I was really uptight. There were tears almost streaming down my face. I was fighting them back, I was so upset. I reviewed all my progress for him. Three new accounts, two sets of gold cufflinks.

* $66,222 a month in rental equipment.

"He said it was out of his hands, told me this bullshit story about it having been decreed higher up. I said I wanted to talk to 'higher up,' who turned out to be a stumbling boob. I went to see him and he told me about the critical situation out there in Queens, then proceeds to try to have me run down all the people I don't like and thought were incompetent over the past year, and bleed me for as much information to fill his little crap kit as he could.

"So I went to see the branch manager out in Queens, and he was an operator if ever there was one. I get this line—'I don't know if I want you in the first place, kid. They're trying to push you down my throat, etc.'

"What's the deal? It's this: two-man sales team, I'm junior man, sixty–forty split on all commissions. I tell him I'm struggling now on $625, I got one kid, a car, trying to buy a house, and he says, 'It's not my problem, and by the way, your salary gets cut to $500.'

"Five hundred dollars? Why? I heard you got to keep your salary if you'd done an outstanding job. I told him about the three new accounts and the two pairs of gold cufflinks. 'Nothing doing,' he said.

"'Ah, but don't forget,' he says. 'Pan Am's your big customer here, and they have a 705 installed. That goes for $40,000 a month; they use it three shifts a day. They pay us $30,000 a month in extra-shift rentals. Get rich off IBM.' I was to get $200–$300 a month on residuals for extra-shift use. I took it. I didn't have a choice."

"So Bill Lloyd and I were a team. There was only one reason for it—the critical sales situation in Queens: to hold Lloyd down. I was a 40 percent load around his neck. So Lloyd had several major accounts put on a sixty-day reservation. I couldn't share in commissions until then, because he'd already done work on the accounts and was just waiting to close."

So the new man faced his territory—not the Man-

hattan plum he had expected, but the vast sprawl of
Queens from which he had sought escape.

He left his gold cufflinks in the dresser drawer at
home and set out to knock on every door in one of the
dreariest, weediest industrial suburbs in America. Paul
described the territory as "nothing but tall grass." The
branch manager said it was "nothing but tall chimneys."

Most of the big customers in the territory were already addicted to data-processing equipment, and keeping up with their future needs was easy to do. With a lot
of time on their hands, Jerry and his partner wormed
through Long Island City and called on prospects. Prospect calls are recorded on the salesman's Monthly Sales
Performance sheets; he gets the blue copy, and the other
colors are scattered about in district and regional offices.
The number of prospect calls are averaged per day, compared to the performance standard by which you are
found wanting or above average.

To the great pleasure of the branch manager, the
team was diligent at prospecting. They blocked out their
prospecting territory and called on every business, re-
gardless of how small or how unlikely their need of data-
processing equipment. Jerry, of course, would go anywhere. Compared to chasing down bald-tire prospects,
this job was a pleasure. Everybody loved IBM.

They made proposals to rinky-dink coffee importers,
metal-utensil companies, food processors, yogurt makers,
and noodle manufacturers. One salesman in another territory in the Queens office sold a computer to a sausage
company by proving that the machine could juggle the
hundreds of items that go into sausage, with their current
market prices, and come up with a recipe that met mini-
mal requirements and was cheaper than they could do it
manually.

On rainy days Jerry could sit at his desk and shuffle
papers and make an extra hundred dollars in commissions. The IBM commission plan was incredibly compli-

cated, and the compensation a salesman received depended to an extent on how he wrote the order. If a man ordered two new tape drives and intended to remove two old ones, Jerry might find he could earn a higher commission by canceling the old ones outright instead of charging them against the new ones. Or he might charge them against another piece of equipment altogether. "One had to be resourceful. The prospecting time was not all wasted." Jerry and his partner sold several new accounts, one a unit-record installation to the Pliable Bagel Company. Pliable had specified that before it changed over to punch cards, the bagel company salesmen had to agree to accept the new system. Most of them were elderly Jewish gentlemen who had been selling bagels for a half century and who might well have taken one look at all that new equipment and said, "Who needs it?" Jerry and Bill had to sit down with each of them to convince them that the new system would be better, and to show them how they would write up their orders in the future. The air was thick with unvoiced skepticism as the day approached for the new system to be installed. Pliable had hired a man to handle the new data-processing equipment, and on the eve of the big day he proudly showed Jerry the punch cards he had run through as a test. All set.

The next day Jerry got an urgent call to go to the bagel company. There awaited him a nervous DP Manager and a sad Mr. Pliable. The punch-card machinery stood idle, the victim of an unknown saboteur. On the eve of its debut, someone had severed the main cable, revealing an intriguing cross-section of hundreds of tiny wires.

The IBM customer engineer said no serious damage had been done and he could have it up and running again in a week. For Jerry, the damage was not in the machine but in the possibility that an old and trusted employee had spoken finally against the tyranny of the punch card. If so, it was possible that Mr. Pliable would sympathize with the saboteur and order the machines out. Jerry had to find out who did it, and he had to find out before Mr. Pliable decided that a little modernization was not worth the price of upsetting his whole sales staff.

A conference was called to discuss the matter, and no sooner had they taken seats when Jerry stood up and announced that he knew the culprit's identity. Great astonishment all around. It was the DP Manager, he said. Jerry remembered the sample invoice he had been shown the day before. Each invoice had the customer's name, what he had bought and in what amounts. And a sub-total, with the word "total" printed alongside the amount. "That machine can't be programmed to print 'total' in that position. He must have hand-punched those cards because he hadn't been able to get the program going. When time ran out on him he cut the cable, figuring that he could have it worked out by the end of the week." They called in the DP Manager, and of course he confessed. End of case.

Most of Jerry's time was spent with Pan American because they were the biggest customer. (There were additional men separate from Jerry's staff whose whole "territory" was Pan Am's reservations department.) When Pan Am's DP equipment broke down, Jerry got an IBM company airplane to pick up the airline's data processors and fly them to Poughkeepsie every evening to use IBM's facilities while the repairs were made.

Jerry also kept an eye on the small details that could grow into big problems. One day he was in the DP room at Pan Am and noticed that there was "garbage" in the revenue print-out. "Garbage" is a data-processing term for gibberish or nonsensical words or figures. In this case, there were a string of incoherent letters where there should have been names. They stopped everything and started to check out the whole system, beginning with the printer, then the tape units. Step by step, hour by hour, they followed the flow of data through the maze of circuitry and boxes and found nothing wrong. They finally worked their way through the whole system until there was nothing more to check except one key-punch machine and the girl who operated it. The machine seemed all right, and with great interest Jerry inquired about the operator. He learned that Pan Am rated key-punch operators by the number of key strokes per hour they typed. This poor girl didn't mean any harm, but knowing that alphabetic material is never verified, she had simply raked her finger across the keys to increase her output rating.

For fifteen months Jerry prospected for new customers in Long Island City and kept his old customers smiling and uncomplaining through a score of large and small crises. In 1961, he was taken out of his territory and promoted to Senior Account Rep for American Airlines. He worked full time on the installation of the new passenger-name-record reservation system at American. SABRE, as the new system was called, was the first on-line, real time computer reservation system. It was a major advance in the airlines industry because it kept an up-to-date record of the passenger's name and his flight information, sharply reducing the incidence of over- and undersold flights. At least, that was what it was going to do when they got it working. When Jerry was transferred to SABRE it wasn't working yet.

In 1962, he was made Operational Programming Manager, and in 1963 he became Project Manager for AA, and by 1964 SABRE was on line.

In the beginning, every time they started the system up and put on the test program, the computers would turn themselves off after the first transaction. Slowly the bugs were found and the system would stay up for a while, though for a whole month it broke down an average of sixty times a day.

The SABRE system was first tested out in a few

cities to see how it would operate under real conditions, and it was down more than it was up. Anything might knock it out, and no explanation could ever be found. A ticket agent might be doing something that was confusing to the computer. In one memorable example, a Boston agent was trying to book seats for a hockey team. Every time he entered the names and requested space, the computer would conk out. Jerry and his staff would bring the computer back up, and the Boston agent would request space, and down it would go. To solve the problem they had to find out which agent was the "mad bomber" so they could analyze what he was doing.

In this case they discovered that the names of the hockey team totaled 244 characters, the last of which was an "n." For some reason, this particular combination killed the computer.

Tempers at American were getting understandably short, and they began to blow on a cold night in the spring of 1963. The computer had sold about 250 seats on a 100-seat plane, leaving 150 people at the gate who watched bitterly as their plane ascended into the night sky without them. They complained loudly and forcefully to American, and an American vice-president screamed at IBM to get those machines out because they would never, never work. Jerry Paul, not yet with sufficient authority to even do so, called a meeting while the bumped passengers were still shaking their fists. The senior executives at American and IBM sat down to court-martial the computer. Jerry got his whole programming staff to stand by in the hall, and he assembled every piece of data that had been fed into the computer concerning that flight. He reviewed each item, brought in his witnesses as they were needed, and after eighteen hours of arguing and examining, the guilt had been evenly distributed. American was partly in error, individual reservations agents were partly in error, as was the computer. Jerry's handling of the incident strengthened his reputation with American, and shortly afterward he was made Project Manager.

Bigger things were waiting for him, and evidence of this came in his selection to attend an exclusive IBM executive-training school at Sand's Point, New York. The purpose of the school is partly training in executive style and partly evaluation.

The value of the class and its importance to one's career at IBM are subjects of debate, but Jerry did well and was appointed class valedictorian, the figurative equivalent to another pair of gold cufflinks. He returned to his job for only a short time before he became Airlines Sales Manager. His territory was the United States, and his quota was a million and a quarter points, or the equivalent in sales of $60 million a year. At the age of thirty-one, he became the first really big-time traveling computer salesman.

Although his official title was that of Sales Manager, Jerry assumed much of the burden of the direct-sales effort himself. In 1965, he covered his coast-to-coast territory by plane as intensively as any trunk peddler ever toured a state by train or horse and buggy. He would leave New York on Monday, drop in to see United in Chicago, switch to Continental Airline to visit their executive offices in L.A. From there he would return to New York via Denver and Dallas. During that whole year he spent five out of seven days on the road—or rather, in the air.

In 1965, Jerry and his wife separated. They were divorced in 1966. He insists that his being away from home all week was not the cause of the divorce. His present wife would strongly object if Jerry began to travel frequently. Without going into the details of the marriage, it is obvious that with the Pauls, as with all families of men who travel, prolonged absence is a hardship on married life.

True to the tradition of traveling men, he became very knowledgeable and preferential about the amenities of travel. Most of his flights were fairly long and between major cities, which meant that there were plenty of extras to choose from in the way of food and entertainment. Since Jerry's customers were the airline executives, he always traveled first-class and with the airline he was going to call on.

"The first thing an airline executive will ask you is how your flight was. And he wants to know, *in detail*. You had better have been flying *his* airline, and you had better have been up front. He wants to hear how you liked the steak, not about franks and beans. After all, IBM was asking a good dollar for its first-class services, so I felt I should purchase first-class service when I flew. Although I got some static about my expense accounts."

Jerry's alcohol consumption doubled under the liquid benevolence of first-class airline travel and the tyranny of the unquenchable thirst of some of the many airline executives his job required him to drink with. The drinking and dining phase of business is more intense during the sales effort, and was especially intense for Jerry since the product he was selling could not be delivered for two years. The customer had to be sold, and he had to stay sold during the time IBM struggled to get its new computer generation—System 360—on the production line. There was a favorite joke during those years about the woman who had married three times and was still a virgin. Her first two marriages had been to a policeman and a fireman, both of whom fell in the line of duty before the marriage was consummated. Her third marriage was to an IBM salesman, and the virgin wife complained that "all he does is sit on the edge of the bed and tell me how great it's going to be." Jerry's job was to sell the new Passenger Airline Reservation System (PARS) and keep the airline executives thinking about how great it was going to be.

There was a considerable amount of hot competition developing among the computer manufacturers over the wide-open airline market. Only the American Airlines' SABRE system was a true passenger-name-record reservation system. Most of the other airlines used a relatively primitive system that kept track of the number of seats available, but could not keep a passenger list. Without being able to check the number of seats against the names of the passengers, the system was prone to error. The other airlines, envious of American's success, were anxious and eager customers for computers, and the task of programming a reservation system seemed simple enough. Jerry knew it was not simple, and to convince his prospects of this he delivered the SABRE dance—a recitation of horror stories about programming, design, and operations. He told them about the month in which the computer went down sixty times a day, about the hockey team with 244 characters ending in "n," and about the plane that took off from Buffalo with enough passengers left at the gate to start a riot. Of the fourteen domestic airlines big enough to use a computerized reservation system, twelve got the beat of SABRE dance and ordered from IBM. The holdouts were TWA and United. United, the biggest domestic airline, felt that they were going to make a great leap forward with a really sexy computer system. They sent out a Request for Proposal to all the computer companies, outlining what they wanted. Jerry and his associates worked day and night to respond, delivering their detailed proposal in a looseleaf notebook about the size of the Manhattan telephone directory—twelve copies as directed. According to a UAL employee, Sperry Rand put together a thirty-volume opus (times twelve) that had to be delivered by a forklift truck.

IBM was eliminated in the first round, when the field of bidders were narrowed to three. United dismissed the IBM bid as a "warmed-over SABRE," then gazed with rapture at the definitive work by Sperry, and bought it.

Jerry's second loss was TWA. The details are locked in the hearts of the few men who made the decision, and no satisfactory explanations were ever made. TWA had informally indicated that they had selected the IBM PARS system, when word came through that they had signed a contract with Burroughs.

For a year, Jerry had done the SABRE dance. Now he learned a new step, popular in the halls of great corporations, called the lateral arabesque. He was moved to Branch Sales Manager for a few months, then reassigned to the Systems Development Division, of which he eventually became Director of Information and Data Processing Systems, in 1968. In 1969, he left IBM with a group of his colleagues and started a computer-services company which has been very successful. His favorite sales tool is still the SABRE dance.

In 1970, United Airlines terminated its contract with Sperry, after having no success in getting their program off the ground. They installed an IBM PARS system to replace their antiquated seat counter. The decision to go with Sperry cost the airline a five-year delay and about $20,000,000 in cash outlay. And according to *Fortune* it cost the president of United his job. TWA has discarded their Burroughs computers as unworkable and has also installed the PARS system. Burroughs and TWA are now in court with countersuits arising from the removal of the BALKY system.

Jerry Paul finally won them all, but too late for him.

Jerry's primary attraction to IBM had been money, and his secondary attraction had been the status. However, these two goals did not exist in isolation, one from the other. Money alone would not have been enough if the job had been degrading in Jerry's eyes.

As it turned out, IBM salesmen were not as well paid as Jerry had imagined, although he earned $48,000 in the year he presided over $60,000,000 worth of sales.

IBM salesmen who earn large commissions are quickly put on salary. There is a popular story in the trade that the IBM salesman who had a stretch of wet sand in his territory called Cape Canaveral suddenly found himself with a substantial amount of commissions due. He was immediately taken off quota and given a raise, but the big commission was never paid. I have heard similar stories from other computer salesmen. The point is that, while sales figures often run high, commissions do not always follow. By way of contrast, Jerry cited a friend of his who sold rubber bands and paper clips, and reported an income of over $100,000 in the same year.

Jerry left IBM with a salary of $40,000, but this was as Director of the Data Processing Systems of the Development Division, not as a salesman. He had recovered from his "lateral reassignment"—demotion—and could have looked forward to more promotions and more money in the future. However, as vice-president of Data Dimensions—the company he helped to found—his stock in the company has a current market value of over $1,000,000. That kind of status and money is hard to beat with the best territory in the world.

However, there wasn't enough room in a small company for two giant egos to thrive—Jerry's and his cofounders—so Jerry collected his contract, played tennis, made wine, grew vegetables, and spent considerable time with his family before becoming Senior Vice-President of the New York City Off-Track Betting Corporation, leaving the road with some reluctance.

Chapter Nine

From Doctor
to Doctor

While Jerry Paul was moving through the upper levels of traveling salesmanship, Owen Taylor, as we shall call him, plodded through the middle ground in a less successful and less rewarding pursuit. Although Owen had had some experience as a retail camera salesman while he was still in college, his first road trip as a salesman was for a company called New Teaching Systems, Inc., a producer of films, books, and visual-aid materials for the medical profession. Owen's product was an audiovisual unit with eight short pediatric films. The films were in a cartridge which could be loaded into the back of a projector with a self-contained screen. It looked like a small television set and, once loaded, could be operated simply by pressing a button. The Patient Guidance Course, as the unit and the films were called, was meant for the waiting rooms of all the pediatricians and hospitals in America. Mothers and small children waiting to see the doctor could be entertained and educated, on such topics as growth and development, toilet training, and dental care. The PGC was leased to the pediatrician for $46 a month for a minimum of twelve months. A signed contract was worth $552 to the company, less the salesman's commission of $46, or one month's rent. If the doctor kept the PGC longer than a year, the salesman would receive an extra commission. When Owen Taylor set out on his first trip, the details of salary and commission had not been fully agreed on, but New Teaching Systems executives imagined that their salesmen, working on salary plus commission, would earn around $20,000 a year.

Owen's first trip was to Philadelphia. In preparing for the trip, he had spent a couple of afternoons on the telephone tracking down doctors, in hospitals and medical schools, who hid behind busy schedules and officious nurses and secretaries. He had a list of five doctors who had responded to either an advertisement or a demonstration of the PGC at a recent convention. He got appointments with all five. Not bad, he thought. And by sheer luck he was able to arrange to see all of them in the same day, beginning at 8:00 in the morning, and finishing in time to catch a train to New York around 5:30.

The sales manager at New Teaching Systems was very firm on appointments. "We want to stay out of the same line with the detail men (pill salesmen from the pharmaceutical companies). "The average belly-to-belly selling time the detail man gets is one and a half minutes. And he gets that by sitting out in the doctor's waiting room or catching him in the hospital corridor. We're asking for ten minutes. By appointment. And I don't think you should go to see him unless you get it, firm."

Owen's first appointment was at 8:00. The doctor showed up with two other doctors and a head nurse, and they were all quite eager to see the films and the self-contained projector.

Owen's first appointment was at 8:00. The doctor into the projector, spoke knowingly, he thought, of the many advantages of the PGC, and then sat back and lis-

tened to objections, the final one being that any purchase
of this size would have to be integrated into the budget
for the coming year. Easy to show. Hard to sell. He had
left the cab driver waiting, since he had an appointment
on the other side of town and the timing was close. He
had stayed longer than he thought, and he found the
cabbie whining to the nurse at the front desk that he had
been waiting for some salesman for over an hour and he
had run out on him. "Some salesman" was the phrase that
grated.

The rest of the day was pretty much the same: everyone very much interested, no one with ready funds. At
the last appointment, the doctor immediately called in a
few junior members of his teaching staff and a colleague.

Owen was the tin peddler reincarnated with shiny
utensils to beguile. They crowded around and nodded
approvingly and leaned forward to see.

"It's really great. We'll sure talk it over." The doctor
hesitated, still looking at the machine, eyes narrowed.
Owen held his breath. It was just like he had read
about. The man was ready to buy. Time to close. Ask for
the order!

"Buy it now," Owen said. "You can make my day."

The doctor marched out of the room and was back
in three minutes. He handed Owen the contract with a
sweep. "I signed it." Owen had to go to the director's
office to find out who to send the bill to. The director
had been on the telephone when the doctor had come
in for the OK, and when Owen arrived he was just
hanging up. The secretary who ran things was going in
circles when she saw the contract and immediately
pounced on the director when he hung up. "Did you see
this? Did you see what Dr. Warton bought?"

"I thought he said it was forty-six dollars," the director said. "Forty-six dollars! It's forty-six dollars a *month*,"
she screamed.

"Oh, that's all right. It looks good," he said blandly.

She turned to, or rather *on*, Owen. "Can we at least *see* the thing?" You'd think it was her money.

"Certainly," he said. He had no intention of giving a demonstration if he could help it. The sale had been made, and a further demonstration could only allow him to keep what he already had or lose it. He had nothing to gain.

The director was reaching for his hat. It was almost five o'clock, and you could hear the traffic outside begin to roar. Owen casually asked the director if he would care to see a few of the films. "Not now," he said over his shoulder. When the secretary turned around, as Owen assumed she did, he was gone.

He headed back to New York rather pleased with himself for his first day out.

On his desk were more letters from pediatricians in various parts of Pennsylvania who had written in for information about the PGC. Owen now had to transform these into solid appointments, and in a sequential pattern that would make it possible for him to call on them.

The telephone ploy was the same: to either get by the nurse or emphasize the doctor's interest in the strongest manner without actually saying that he asked someone to call. Owen didn't want to sound like another salesman trying to sell the doctor. In fact, no one ever wants to sound like a salesman to a doctor.

He managed to line up the appointments in an orderly enough fashion to conform to his itinerary, and on Monday morning he set out. A more experienced salesman who drives a car for a living surely does have air conditioning and probably does not have a VW. The drive to Philadelphia was a two-hour sauna amid bouncing trucks and tailgating buses, and Owen's eyes burned from the fumes that shroud the New Jersey Turnpike. To follow the signs to downtown Philadelphia is impossible. Most of them are an offhand gesture, ignored by people who know the way, and confusing to those who don't.

He had two calls to make that were for demonstrations and would not produce any immediate sales. Nonetheless, he hoped that somehow he could sell something, and he pleasantly daydreamed about it. He wondered if it went with being a salesman. Do the good ones or the bad ones daydream?

The two demonstrations turned out to be just that. One was a medical school, and the other was to the Pennsylvania Medical Association—just to keep them informed about new developments in the field of medical communications.

It was a dull day with a lot of driving, and he was glad to head for the most comfortable motel he could find. He made a bad choice and learned a valuable lesson. It's better not to have a room in a motel at the foot of a hill, if it's too close to the highway. Trucks rumbled through his room all night, gearing down going east, revving up going west. By morning he felt as if he had tossed on the highway all night.

He drove most of the day and arrived in Johnstown, Pennsylvania, around four o'clock in the afternoon and checked into a Holiday Inn, which after many years of travel has come to look like home to most salesmen. He checked the yellow pages and called all the pediatricians in town, made four appointments for the next day and one immediately. Quick work, he thought.

The building was easy to find, being the only new building in a gray industrial ghetto. There were two doctors in practice together, and they were giving shots. Owen hustled down and set up the machine with the immunization film. He put it on the table in the reception room. The nurses ignored Owen and the film. Parents and children stopped and watched. Some interest developed. One father asked the nurse if this was something new they had added, or was it on trial. "Jus sumpin he's got," she said, tilting her head in Owen's direction. He smiled and nodded, recalling advice from an old book on trading with the Indians: "Smile so they will know you're friendly."

Finally the two sour-faced doctors came out to see what the slicker was trying to put over on them. Owen explained the purpose of the PGC and demonstrated how simple it was to operate, and they backed away as if it was going to get them. "It'll answer a lot of questions patients may call you to ask at midnight," Owen said.

"It'll just make 'em think of new questions to ask," said one. They both slapped their knees in sudden mirth.

Tomorrow will be better. Owen went back to the motel tired and hungry. He ate in the Matador Room, named apparently for the print, hanging on the wall, of a girl similar to the one on the Maja soap wrapping. There was also a picture of a bullfight. He had an over-cooked steak, a glass of chilled red wine, and a cup of instant coffee.

Johnstown is a tight little community in the hills. Owen sensed that it was not the place to sell newfangled gadgets, and the run of the day's interviews proved him right. He saw every pediatrician in town, and their general reaction was that the last traveling salesman they saw sold them a wooden nutmeg or a clock that wouldn't run. They met him with open suspicion and began to say "I don't want any" before they understood what he was selling.

The salesman's creed holds that he must accept every "no sale" as a personal error, the direct result of negative thinking, wrong opening gambit, or failure to close properly. Owen silently confessed that he was not optimistic about tomorrow. Even from his brief experiences he could already understand why salesmen begin to tell themselves stories, trying to convince themselves of the rightness of what they are selling. In the act of selling you must believe. You have to believe that what you are saying is true, at least for that moment. All day he had heard doctors complain that the PGC was too expensive.

He did not think so when he began to sell it, but now they had convinced him that it was.

He found himself remembering phrases from how-to-go-get-'em sales books. If he were to make a sale while remembering some hint or rule, it would become a talisman to be evoked on future occasions, and a secret belief in the metaphysics of selling would begin to form. In time, the salesman comes to believe there are powers, perhaps unholy ones, that lurk about, ready to work in his service or conspire against him.

He had one more call to make in Johnstown and he had already written the sales report. He explained in the report why the doctor did not buy. He did it for the same reason a man who wants rain might wash his car.

The last visit, as prophesied, was a washout. The doctor was about eighty, had cut his practice back to ten patients a day, and was about to retire. He watched one of the films with patience and kind humor. "You see the other doctors here in town?"

"Yes."

"You sell 'em?"

"No, it's hard."

"Yes, I know it is."

It was the first time in three days anyone had spoken to him as a person and not as "some salesman." He was grateful.

He checked into a motel and called home. His daughter was sick last night. His wife called the doctor, who was out of town. The substitute doctor said that with a temperature of 105 degrees she should see a doctor, but he said he couldn't come. He couldn't see her before 3:00 tomorrow afternoon. If she's still alive. Son of a bitch. His wife called another doctor, who came and gave her a couple of aspirins, and a bill for $25.

Owen slept peacefully through all this, having found a quiet motel away from truck noises. This was a typical situation in families whose men travel. Wives cope alone and husband returns, wanting to be comforted and welcomed.

In the morning, men pour out of the motel rooms like troops into the company street. They escape into breakfast and newspapers, then off to the day's work. Their cars peel out of the driveway and into the morning sun that skims the expressway—a vast, energetic army armed with credit cards and propelled by rented cars, housed in motels, comforted by strangers.

Owen could see how life on the road could even be exhilarating for a really successful traveling salesman— storming into town, writing up a few big orders, and then off to new conquests. The second time around it might be a little less glorious.

He had a call to make in Beaver Falls, a town every bit as ingrown as Johnstown. Every time he had called the doctor there for an appointment he was out or busy, so Owen was going to sit on his doorstep. He had decided that he had been showing the wrong film and he had chosen another one whose general theme was, "Don't worry; leave everything to the doctor because he knows what he's doing." The doctor ought to appreciate that. And he had also decided that he had been a little too stiff in his presentation and should unbend a little.

The presentation was better. The doctor really liked the Growth and Development film. "All children are different," it says. "Your child is different. Don't worry about a thing, because your doctor is well-trained. Mothers, relax."

He said he would talk to his partner and let Owen know. Owen said, "Thank you, and I'll be looking forward to hearing from you." He knew already that he had lost the sale.

Meadville was next, in the northwestern part of the state. The town was more prosperous. It was quieter and cleaner than the industrialized satellites of Pittsburgh. He was running a little ahead of schedule, but he couldn't change the appointment because the doctor was busy. He checked into a motel and began to look around for something to do. The pool halls had all gone out of business, and the only movie was a Disney boy-meets-dog.

The town is proud of its history, founded in the late 1700s, and the homes are old, stately, and set amid heavy oak trees and spacious lawns. He sat for a while on a park bench by the courthouse, surrounded by acres of green grass, four churches, a high school, a National Guard post, and various memorials to fallen heroes, one of whom had been burned at the stake by the Indians. The houses that fill the spaces between the aforementioned institutions are Victorian gingerbread and carpenter gothic.

Sitting there by the cannon and a pile of silvered cannon balls, watching the sun play against the tops of the trees and the far side of the park, it seemed that here was one of those towns that had fallen out of step with the march of time. But Owen noticed that someone had poured blood-red dye over the silvered cannon balls, undoubtedly as a war protest, though the point was probably lost on most of the citizenry. And he heard that evening that seven students in a local college had been arrested for smoking pot.

The next morning he took the car to a car wash and got the wax-spray job, vacuumed rocks and dirt out of the inside, cleaned all the windows, polished the hub caps. All set.

The traveling salesman lives in chaos, so everything he can give order to is so ordered. Fresh shirt, haircut, shined shoes, clean shave. Clean car. All set. Just so. Because by the end of the day he's rumpled and oily and tired and baggy. He has to keep up his own morale because most of the time he works alone.

After what seemed like half his life, the day passed and he waited in the reception room for his last chance of the week. The doctor came in, late, regarded Owen but did not speak, and walked over to the machine. Owen introduced himself and began to explain the PGC and briefly extol its merits. He had received no indication as yet that the doctor was not totally deaf. He played the film about the mothers, not worrying, and the doctor watched it without comment. When it was over, Owen said, "Why don't you try it for twelve months?" The doctor said he would. Owen flipped out a contract, and he signed it.

The sales report asked, "What closed the sale?" "*You* tell *me*," Owen thought.

Owen Taylor did not last as a salesman, and the PGC did not last as a product. The films survived and are now sold, at a greatly reduced price, for regular slide projectors. They are sold by telephone. It gave Owen some passing satisfaction that the company found that the doctor's greatest complaint about the PGC was the expense.

Chapter Ten

From Door to Door

There were balloons on the wall and a picture of Christ. Fifteen men sat squeezed together on a row of folding chairs. Their nervous, loud voices carried over the scratchy recorded music: pre-Musak combinations of military marches and Broadway-belt-em-outs. They waited.

There was Growitz. Top seller, rumored to make close to $30,000 a year—a pudgy, tough former welder, looking uncomfortable in a starched white-collared shirt, one size too small.

And Hicks, another good salesman, but the opposite of Growitz in dress and temperament, with baggy gray pants, like a circus clown, white socks and brown shoes, unpolished. He could fit a bottle of rug shampoo into his back pocket—a quart-size bottle, not those little four-ounce samples. His hair appeared to have been cut with shears and oiled. The nap ran to the front and there was no part. Hicks was a boomer and back slapper. He said "Oh boy" a lot and ran around the room greeting everyone as they came in. Or he did before they started waiting.

Sudden quiet. *He* was coming down the hall. Fifteen chairs slid back to the wall, clacking. Feet scuffled, now stomped in cadence. They clapped their hands. Al Wilson, his first day on the job, found himself sitting in a roomful of grown men who had just jumped to their feet and started clapping and singing "We're going to sell, sell, sell." Wilson felt like he was in someone else's church and didn't know how the service went, and what he could figure out he couldn't bring himself to do.

The sales manager was here. His turn to say something funny. The singing ended with general applause and laughter as all eyes turned to him. "You guys should burn that energy out on those doorbells instead of wasting it here." All laughed. He made it. They knew he would. Real joke is that he was the enforcer of morale and enthusiasm, and he made them clap and sing, and he pretended that it was all their bursting spirit. Over him were bigger enforcers that made sure he made them clap and sing. It was company policy. There was a lot of that in the door-to-door vacuum-cleaner business.

It all happened fast. Sacher, the sales manager, blond curly hair, big smile, spun the roulette—a numbered bike wheel with nails. "Let's see which one a youse is lucky this mornin. Eleven! Charley, who's eleven? Simpson! Oh, boy, here's a prospect." Charley was keeper of attendance. You got a number when you came in. If your number won you got a prize or a name of a prospect you could call on that day.

Now for the balloons. You got a balloon for selling a B-8. That was a tile and carpet beautifier. Hicks had two, so he got two balloons. Inside was a piece of paper that told him what he won. "Oh boy." He could take any two things he saw on the wall. He took the picture of Christ and a truck driver's wallet—the kind you can keep in your back pocket and hook to your belt. "Oh boy, that's real leather." He and Sacher did a put-on dialogue.

"Yeah. Coulda got plastic, you know. Nothing too good for my men." Company policy.

Now down to business. Hicks was to demonstrate how he made his Model G sale yesterday. Sales manager and Growitz were to act as man and wife.

Wife: "I have a Hoover."

Hicks: "I thought he was in the White House? I guess that was a long time ago. Yeah, those were sure good machines, all right." He ran the vacuum over the rug as he talked.

Wife: "We're not interested in a new machine right now." Hicks continued to vacuum the rug, ignoring the protest. He took the dust bag from the machine and began to dump it on the carpet into neat little piles.

Wife: "I can't understand where all that dirt came from. I'm a good housekeeper."

Hicks is comforting. "It's all right. You did the best you could with that old machine." He took out a crevice tool, went around the chair, vacuumed up a moth or palmed it in the bag—hard to say which.

Hicks: "Oh boy, look at that. I'll bet your husband sleeps in that chair too, with his mouth open. What you need is the mothball vaporizer attachment. Of course, you can just keep a jar of mothballs around and throw them at moths if you see one. What's your first name, Mrs. Prospect?"

Wife: "Why, Florence, but we don't want to buy a machine just now."

Hicks: "And this is 110 Elm Street." He went on filling out the form over her protest. Applause. You could almost see the curtain fall.

Sacher was on his feet. "Now, you see what Hicks did? Did he listen to one damn word she said? You bet he didn't. And did you notice he made her sit down right by her husband. Why? So he can keep his eye on them. Don't you leave them alone for a minute. Don't you let them out of sight for a minute to signal to the other. The minute that happens, the husband shakes his head or signals 'no' and you're dead. From then on, you might as well be back on the sidewalk. That's all! Now, what are you going to do?" There was general clatter. Fifteen men were on their feet, clapping, singing, "Sell, sell, sell."

Wilson, the new man, on his first day, was to go out with Johnny Caspo, a former life-insurance salesman in the lower middle of the sales chart. They made a service call first thing at the Catholic Church. Machine, Model G with power nozzle, popped open when bag was less than half full. Johnny listened gravely to the women at church describe the symptoms. Solemnly he opened the end with a screwdriver, found nothing wrong, put it back together. He tried the old bag. The machine popped open. The machine wasn't supposed to pop open until the bag was full. That was the automatic part of the Automatic Model G. He tried a new bag and the machine worked fine. They made a lot of cement around Allentown and it got into everything; fine heavy gray dust. It clogged up the pores in the bag, and the machine popped open. Johnny delivered a rambling discourse on vacuum cleaners. The women eyed him rather sympathetically. They understood. He didn't know how the thing worked either.

"This is a Catholic town. If I don't take care of this church, I'm dead in this town," he told Wilson when they were outside.

So they started out to sell, to actually begin to ring doorbells and ask, seriously ask, every woman who opened her door if she would like to spend about $185 this morning on a vacuum cleaner with all the attachments. It was a hard way to make a living. Like Grade B symbolism, it started to drizzle. It was cold.

Wilson waited in the car, and Johnny tried four
doors before he got in. Wilson came in carrying the
machine and sat in the corner quietly.

The wife and two kids sat on the sofa and watched
Johnny clean the rug and make the little piles of dirt.
It wasn't working like the skit Hicks did this morning.

Johnny took the little piles of dirt and, in despera-
tion, made one big pile: "Look, missus, all that dirt came
out of your rug. Now, missus, I know you do the best
you can with your old machine and you really care
about the health of your children, so don't you think
you should have this machine?" She gazes, somewhat
abstractly, at the enormous pile of gray fuzz.

"There're a lot of things I want before a new vacuum
cleaner."

"Now, missus, I'm sure your husband insists on good
tools. What does he do for a living?" A good ploy, but
it was the wrong question. Her husband ran an elevator
in the cement plant.

The kids loved it. They oohed and ahhed over
each pile of dirt Johnny wrung out of the demo bag. He
sucked up white cloths so fast they seemed to vanish.
The kids giggled as the machine lifted three one-pound
steel balls in a superb show of strength. Not a flicker
from the woman. A wandering minstrel had performed
for the kids, free. A hell of a lot of things she wanted
before she would buy a $185 vacuum cleaner.

Down a row of frame houses, two-family, pressed
together, rickety, decaying. Johnny, the seer: "There's
money in this neighborhood. Look at them shacks. They
gotta be paid off already. How much could they be? Like
you go into a new neighborhood. Young couples, just
bought the house. Everything brand new. No money.
They owe it all."

Six more houses before a hit, then they were in.
The woman screamed at her children and smiled at them.
Sure, they could come in and clean her kitchen floor.

Johnny was very big on the Model B-8. She let him demonstrate the waxer by doing her whole floor, kept him going with questions, and then wandered out of the room when he was almost finished. When she came back Johnny was on his knees for his big line. "This machine will keep you off your knees."

"I got one somethin like it already," she said.

He told her about the contest and how he could win a hundred-dollar bond to help put his boy through college someday if she only bought this machine. But the floor was waxed and she didn't give a crap about his contests. Wilson helped her put the furniture back in place. A look of distance had congealed over her eyes. In her mind she had moved on to other things.

This went on all day. Johnny stopped snapping his fingers and saying, "Man it can change just like (snap) that." It was raining again and it had been a long time since he clapped his hands to sell, sell, sell. At the next stop he got excited again because he was going to sell the whole thing—the Model G and the B-8 and the power nozzle. This was his neighborhood. He waved to his son who was just passing, going home from school. He whistled up the walk as they brought everything in from the car. He spoke German with the old couple and told all the children how this was going to get Mom off her knees. Everybody thought the rug shampooer was the greatest thing since automobiles. They thought it was so great they got him to clean a couple of rugs. Then it came. The mortgage was due. The car was in the shop. The kids needed clothes.

Like damp cold settling into stiff joints, bitterness crowded itself into the consciousness of Johnny Caspo.

On the way home, he talked about the way dishonest salesmen drove him out of the insurance business and how other vacuum-cleaner salesmen from his own office had lied to his prospects to steal sales from him. But the worst ones were the people. They lied to you. They said they'd buy but you never heard from them. They'll tell you anything.

When a salesman isn't selling, it's a sad thing to see. Wilson thought they would hustle up and down the street until the last house turned out the lights. But by five o'clock Johnny Caspo was through.

Every day, Monday through Saturday, the Cyclomatic salesmen meet in the little sales office on South Main Street in Elmwood. Their brothers hold similar meetings all over the country and sing variations of the same songs and roar into the day with the same zip. "Roar" is a good verb this month. The *Cyclomatic News* headlines: "Tiger, Tiger on the Trail/Out To Get Another Sale/ Tracking Hard With All His Might/Sure To Score/Again Tonight."

This month you can win the Royal Bengal Tiger Tie Tac for only Ten Sales. (Handsome Custom-Made Special Gifts from Vice-President Hardy Sercle. GGRRR! GET GOING, TIGER! GGRRR!)

Wilson showed up at the sales office at eight as directed. No one else showed up until around half past, and the meeting began at a quarter of nine. He was at a loss to explain why he was misled about the time or why he was unwitting enough not to remember the starting time from the day before.

Sacher had a cracked tooth, Wilson overheard as he lounged around the salesroom in the pre-Sousa quietness. Sacher's usually forced joviality was really being ground out today. He left for the dentist, and the field manager conducted the morning revival. Wilson was again trapped, not wanting to offend, but unwilling to throw himself into the thing. He also had trouble clapping his hands in the predawn trot around boot camp. Some things you never grow out of. Yancy sold two cleaners yesterday and was invited to tell the others how he did it. He sold both with the carpet beautifier attachment.

Yancy had one trick that probably only he and

Growski would pull. (Both had worked at the steel mill
and were a little more aggressive than some of the other
salesmen. Perhaps working by the hour at a hard, dirty
job had generated a sincere desire to avoid it if possible.) Yancy was a bantam rooster, with a cowlick that
rose over his head like a crown. He jumped around the
room piling up mounds of dust, snapping the demo bag
until they were all coughing, tasting, smelling dust. The
field manager brought out a small piece of carpet so
Yancy could demonstrate the rug shampooer. Yancy rejected it. He preferred to clean a small spot in the center
of the big rug. He glanced wildly around the room as he
started up the shampooer. "They always say, 'My god,
you aren't going to just leave that spot in the middle, are
you?' And I say, 'Oh no, I'll clean the whole rug right
after the sale.'" He must have been thrown out of a lot of
homes for that stunt. "I get a real white circle right in the
middle of a gray rug. It looks just like the moon
coming up. I'll always tell 'em that."

Sid Skinner was to be Wilson's teacher that day. Skinner was a very mild-mannered fellow, about fifty-five, and
crewcut. He had been with Cyclomatic for many years,
leaving for a short time for an inside selling job with
Hess Brothers. Skinner was in the middle of the sales
chart, and amid all the wild talk about fantastic earnings
as a door-to-door salesman, Wilson noted that Skinner
made $8200 last year. This was not a salary to be ashamed
of, but it wasn't the heady wage implied in much of the
literature.

They headed north to Allentown again. South of
here the towns were smaller, more rural. The houses
were scattered and it was hard to make much time. There
weren't any good housing developments until you got to
Doylestown, and that was covered pretty well out of
Philadelphia. Again the weather was bad, this time snow,
turning to rain and back to snow.

Wilson went on ahead to wait at a diner near the

thruway exit while Skinner ran a few errands for his wife, who was in the hospital with a broken hip.

The waitress was genially nosey about what Wilson was doing hanging around there so early in the morning with apparently no place to go. He finally confirmed that he was meeting someone. Sid arrived at 11:30, but he didn't want to start right away because it was getting too close to lunch, so they rode around until 1:00. There were no territories staked out as the private domain of any salesman. They went where they wanted to. There was no systematic approach, such as block by block, house by house. They cruised around while Sid looked for a house that looked good to him. He passed up one street because the traffic was heavy, another because "no one looks home." He wasn't looking for anything he could describe. He was playing a hunch, a quiet, un-admitted game of roulette—Dear Lord, let me hit a hot one.

In the door first try. Amazing. Roulette worked. Old couple lived there, man retired. He used to work for Mack Truck. The woman was on crutches, broken hip. She was watching one of those ghoulish daytime serials drenched with organ music. She and Sid swapped stories about hospitals and doctors while he kept laughing and piling the dirt. (You have to be enthusiastic and keep smiling. These are two of seven rules Skinner had taped to his dashboard, just over a can of dog repellent, much used.) No sale. The man kept saying, "We're on pension. We don't want to buy nothing." He only let them in be-cause Skinner told him about the contest and how he (Skinner) got a couple of bucks for making the demo, which wasn't true.

This was a two-family house. The next door opened two inches. The woman there hadn't time, didn't want anything, had a million things to do. Skinner kept talk-ing, talked his way in. "Just watch the demo and get a chance to win a prize," and softly, "I get a couple of bucks for showing the cleaner." Translation: For a few minutes of your time, you can win a lot of money and I get a few crumbs. What kind of person are you, to deny me a few crumbs?

There *was* a contest. There was always some kind of contest. This month you could win $2500 or two weeks in Paris if you sent in a card saying you saw a demo. You had a chance, but it was a slim one.

They're dripping wet. She was still saying no. She was willing to sign the card. He needn't get the machine out. He ignored her. Once he had her seated, he piled the dirt around her. (If you could surround them with it, they couldn't move.)

Ah! Contact. Her husband is a salesman. Always worked on straight commission. Straight commission is tough, but you can make more money if you are a go-getter. They reminisced about the Depression, life on straight commission, and how it was.

She told him how much she'd like to buy it and help him out. She knows how tough it is. He's telling her how much it would cheer his wife if he could call the hospital and tell her he got enough sales to win the contest and how they can have a nice vacation.

Sid saw a picture of a young man in a silver frame on the table. "Ah, now, there's a handsome go-getter."

"That was our son, only child. He died five years ago."

The momentum of "always be cheerful" was hard to halt in its tracks, and Skinner, nodded, smiling, "Did he really?" as if he had been told that the boy had once played the lead in the school play.

"He was brilliant, just brilliant. He was in medical school. He just got sick and died."

A man works all his life selling on straight commission and his only child dies in early manhood. What is left here that they hang on to?

Skinner dropped Wilson off at the diner where he

left his car. A long day and nothing sold. In a last burst, Skinner jumped out of his car and, over Wilson's protests, cleaned the ice from his windshield.

The waitress in the diner remembered Wilson from this morning. Sounding like his mother asking if he'd been smoking, she said, "Well, you're out here selling something. What is it?"

His first instinct was to lie. He wanted to say that he was doing market research, or an opinion survey, anything.

"Vacuum cleaners. Want to buy one?"

"You gotta be kidding. And how many did you sell today?"

Again the impulse to lie. "None."

She shook her head when he left: "You ought to get a job."

The morning sales meeting had begun when Wilson arrived. Hicks was already showing how his big sale was made. Dust was flying. Today was the first day of spring, and they were to feature a once-a-year double trade-in. You halve the normal rate and then "double" it for the "special." If the customer bought the Model G he got ten dollars for his old machine—provided it was a Cyclomatic. If it was a "foreign" make—anything other than a Cyclomatic—they only gave you six. The junkman picks them up next morning, at a nickel a pound.

Sacher gave out samples of rug shampoo. Today they were to push the shampoo attachment. "Youse gotta show the shampooer. It'll pay your expenses for the year." He did a simple multiplication on the blackboard, showing how, if they sell one shampoo attachment for every four vacuum cleaners, they could make enough to pay their gas and oil for the year. "You always show it, don't you, Hicks?"

Hicks was still vacuuming. "I didn't used to. I didn't used to. But, oh boy, I saw how it brought in more commissions. Now I do. Now I show it. Yes sir!"

The sales manager knew better. Everyone there had *heard* Hicks say he never showed the shampoo attachment. The B-8, yes. That's the separate machine for carpets and tile. But the attachment cost only $40, and the commission on that, for a credit sale, was only $8.

After they clapped hands and sang, Sacher pulled Wilson aside and gave him a little talking to about getting to the meetings on time. Wilson was contrite.

The time had come for Wilson to ring doorbells. Actually, he took yesterday off and skipped the meeting and went to Doylestown. He tried a few houses and copped out.

Pete Vanz was the field trainer. It was his job to take the new salesmen out and supervise them. They headed for South Hills, a suburb of Allentown. Vanz picked this spot because neither Wilson nor the other new men lived near here. Experience has shown that new men go home when they get discouraged. Wilson told him this was probably so.

There, the enemy—stretched out in acres of rows, in white boxes camouflaged by clipped hedges.

Wilson started down the first street, nurturing indifference to hope, fear, or anxiety, hoping at least for some mindless enthusiasm that would get him past the door. No one home. No one home. (Like the old comedian, "I hope, I hope, I hope.")

"I got one already." (Blunt, factual.)

"We wouldn't be interested." (Pretentious.)

"I just bought a new one." (Outright lie, but skillful.)

"We got two." (Truth, equally skillful.)

No answer. (Saw him coming.) He saw the curtain move. He could hear the TV. He rang again. They stayed away, keeping to the back part of the house until they heard the gate click shut.

And once out of the darkness came a red-eyed man, his face heavy with sleep, probably home from the swing shift at the steel mill, pulling his bathrobe around him.

This great hulk said no, and Al Wilson hurried the hell out of there.

He was getting nowhere. He changed his approach. "We're visiting your neighborhood today to demonstrate" . . . be kind to visitors, dammit. He changed. "You can win two weeks in Paris" to "two weeks with De Gaulle." Little joke, no one got it. He went back to straight line.

Don't crowd the door. Remember to step back, smile, show enthusiasm. Enthusiasm. Boy, was he sick of enthusiasm.

Two hours of this. Step back, smile at hostile faces, suspicious, guarded. Once, through the amber door glass, the militant face of an old white-haired out-of-focus woman appeared. Eyes looked at Wilson, down at power nozzle, and she retreated into blackness without even a shake of her head. He felt like a specimen under glass.

This morning they marched around and sang. Now they regrouped, a small routed army, and retreated to the Fornal Diner for lunch.

Vanz said, "People are a bunch of liars. The longer you're in this business you'll see that. Half of them won't even answer the door. And they'll tell you anything." Unfair to salesmen who stand at the door ready to intrude upon the morning quiet. He was bitter, like Johnny.

After lunch—Wilson had scraps of roast beef on white bread—they attacked the newer part of South Hills, a classic middle-class suburb of television commercials. Wilson expected to find women busily comparing detergents and sipping instant coffee, while kids screamed for more pork sausage. They should be real suckers for vacuum cleaners that got deep down dirt out of costly wall-to-wall carpeting. From the top of the hill down to the end of the last street, grass was 1¾ inches high and the shrubs were clipped to box or globe. The doorbell was located by the wrought-iron mailbox and had a light on it. (The little white plastic button lights up.) And it chimes, bing bong. The housewife answered promptly.

None of this hanging back behind the shades, lurking in the darkness.

Just like on TV, she had short hair that was somehow swept upward, and wore slightly baggy pedal pushers (plaid) or a full-pleated skirt hemmed at the knee.

Wilson said his bit. She pleasantly said no. He elaborated, thinking he was close. She pleasantly said no. The middle-class suburban housewife of middle-class South Hills was no sucker. She was a pro. She had heard it all before. Hearing it again didn't make her mad or intrigue her to buy. She had accepted her role as target, or guinea pig, willing to be canvassed and surveyed and solicited, perhaps to the point of expecting it as a guarantee of her position. On the other side of South Hills, Wilson got a somewhat thick-skin attitude about his approach, however fruitless. One woman finally got very angry when he went on about the Cyclomatic when she had just told him she had just bought a new vacuum cleaner. What the hell, everybody has a vacuum cleaner. That's not the point. He was selling *this* vacuum cleaner. He was not selling the desirability of vacuum cleaners, in general, or trying to anticipate that this is the day someone awoke and decided they had to have a vacuum cleaner.

In the week and a half he spent with Cyclomatic, he went out to sell on five days. He made some demos, or as they say, he "piled dirt." But he sold only one machine, and that was to his wife. Except for this dubious triumph, he neither sold, nor saw anyone else sell, a vacuum cleaner.

He left home every morning before eight and got home after eight at night. It seemed that during that time his whole life was centered around vacuum cleaners. The brief time he spent at home with his family seemed to grow shorter every day. He realized that the men who sold vacuum cleaners and were good enough at it to make money, really like it. He would never sell like Growitz and Hicks. He'd be another Sid Skinner, just surviving and straining to do that. He went by the sales office and turned in his equipment. The sales manager was out, but the office secretary was there, and when he told her he was quitting, she didn't seem very surprised. Most of the men who, for one reason or another, try their hand at selling vacuum cleaners door to door will wash out.

In fact, most men who try to become salesmen will, like Owen Taylor and Al Wilson, end up in some other business.

Chapter Eleven

God Bless You, Little Billy

While the big-corporation salesman sits back in his seat on the jet and swirls his martini, life goes on in the mud below. Comparatively speaking, the man deepest in the mire is the house-to-house canvasser, although he is not, as many people suppose, part of a dying breed. Old-fashioned though door-to-door selling might seem, it is not on the wane.

In a study of a group of direct salesmen, Raymond Ries concluded that "door-to-door selling may be distinguished by what might be called its 'classic' character. It cleaves to the prototype of the American salesman—the flamboyant, highly individualistic 'knight of the road,' and it exhibits in an attenuated form those characteristics typical for all selling occupations."[1]

The door-to-door salesman, whose existence is a wonder in the presence of such products of the retailing revolution as shopping centers and discount houses, is a throwback to an earlier form of traveling man.

That first door-to-door salesman—the Yankee peddler
—owed his existence to a general scarcity of goods, lack
of transportation, and the isolation of his customers in the
back country.

The "agents" of the late 1800s and early 1900s, like
O. Henry's Gentle Grafters, lived more by their wits. They
canvassed neighborhoods across the land, peddling their
homemade concoctions of glue, soap, stain removers, stove
polish, and patent medicines, along with miraculous gadg-
ets-that-work-wonders, books, plants and shrubs, worth-
less stocks and bonds, and franchises.

Mass production, freight trains, and the automobile
have made selling on the doorstep obsolete. Even the
sales spiel, that vital face-to-face confrontation with the
consumer, has been usurped by the radio and television
announcer. Housewives who sought to bar the salesman
from the door were startled to discover that he had ma-
terialized behind them, right in the middle of their living
room. First, radio brought only his voice, then television
brought his form. The sight of a family gathered around
watching television commercials would excite the envy of
any snake-oil peddler or lightning-rod agent who ever
lived.

Robert Heinlein, the science-fiction writer, described
a future world in which the hucksters on billboards and
television screens could shove products right into the
viewer's face. We await only a few refinements in holog-
raphy to wake to this reality.

It is his anachronistic nature that tends to make the
door-to-door salesman today a somewhat comic and pa-
thetic character to the popular mind, best known for his
habit of sticking his foot in your door.

There was, of course, a time when the door-to-door
salesman was trained to begin his sales spiel as soon as
the door opened, while simultaneously placing his foot on
the threshhold. One book salesman, recalling his early
days, said the lady of the house once slammed the door

on his foot with such force that he limped for a week.[2] Door-to-door men today are taught not to crowd the door, and to take a step backwards when it is opened, but a reputation once gained is hard to lose.

The salesman still comes to your door, whether you need him or not. In the face of his economic obsolescence, he thrives. There are today more than two million people ringing doorbells to sell, according to the estimates, about $4 billion worth of goods. Over 66,000 companies are engaged in direct selling.

One of the most successful direct-sales companies is Avon Products, and it is the largest cosmetic company in the world. Avon was founded in 1886 by David H. McConnell, a door-to-door book salesman from Oswego, New York, who gave the ladies a free vial of perfume to gain free entrance to the parlor, where he could extol the merits of *Pilgrim's Progress* and *The American Book of Home Nursing*. The perfume was more interesting to the ladies than either of the books, and McConnell decided he should be in the perfume business. He started the California Perfume Company, located in Brooklyn. He later changed the name of the company to Avon, the Shakespearian overtones being more pleasing to a former literary man.

Today, Avon has 450,000 salesladies in the United States, Canada, and fifteen foreign countries. The salesladies (there might be a few men among them, but an Avon spokesman said she didn't know of any offhand) usually are housewives who sell in their own neighborhoods for a few hours a day, and earn only a few thousand dollars a year on their 40 percent commission, but it adds up to more than $759 million a year in gross sales for Avon, a figure that has grown steadily over the years.

The solid growth and profits of many door-to-door companies have made them popular with investors, particularly during recessions, when consumer sales are generally down. The unemployed often turn to selling door-

to-door, and *Barrons* noted that during the layoffs in 1959
caused by the steel strike, vacuum-cleaner sales went
up.[3] During the 1970–71 slump, Electrolux sales increased
at a time when consumer spending was off on everything.
Many engineers who lost their jobs in the economic im-
plosion of the space industry found down-to-earth employment selling vacuum cleaners.

One of the fastest-growing direct-sales companies
is Amway, founded in 1959 by two door-to-door salesmen. Within eight years they had 80,000 men out selling
$50 million worth of goods. They made it look easy, but
Korvette and Helene Curtis both lost money when they
tried to break into the door-to-door business. Korvette got
out altogether, but Helene Curtis is still trying. They
abandoned their attempt to establish their "studio girls"
in Europe and Canada, but sales in this country are now
reported to be good.

Most companies who depend on door-to-door sales do
relatively little consumer advertising. But Culligan, Inc.,
makers of water conditioners, combined a national advertising campaign with aggressive direct selling, and between 1961 and 1965, according to *Business Week* magazine, they doubled their sales. Until 1959, few housewives
had ever heard of a water softener. Then Culligan hit on
the "Hey, Culligan Man!" slogan, uttered in a high-
pitched voice, and sales began to move. The advertising
campaign presold the salesman, rather than the product,
the benefits of which are as difficult to describe as they
are relative. Residents of the commuting towns of northern New Jersey were good customers for water softeners,
even though their water isn't hard. It only *seemed* hard in
comparison to the soft water in New York City.

Culligan men make their appointments during the
day with the housewife, and their sales in the evening,
when the husband is at home. Once inside the door, the
hard sell begins, with stress on vanity appeals to the wife
(shinier hair, cleaner dishes) and the savings on soap to

her husband. The machine sells for $300–$400, which is a lot of soft soap.

In spite of its surprising growth, door-to-door selling in the past has been suited for the more limited role of introducing new products. Most major appliances were introduced into the home by door-to-door salesmen. (The first refrigerator salesmen headed for the old icebox drip pan and talked about germs.) As a means of regular distribution, door-to-door selling is outmoded and overpriced.

A former vice-president of a pots-and-pans company declared that "door-to-door selling is, by its nature, inefficient and expensive, and can only be paid for through prices that are substantially higher than for comparable merchandise in a retail store."[4] His firm sold pots and pans for "at least double" the store price.

William H. Whyte pointed out that "By every rule of scientific marketing, direct canvassing is so patently uneconomic that it has no place in the new era. Yet, while retailers were advertising and promoting and price-cutting in a vain attempt to halt dropping sales, the country's door-to-door salesmen (who don't even mention price if they can help it) closed as many sales in 1951 as they did in 1950—and this despite a severe drift of personnel into less arduous work."[5]

A study of door-to-door selling made back in 1926 concluded that "So far as we have been able to find, there are no articles being sold from house to house which are sold to the consumer at a lesser price than that for which he or she could buy the same or equivalent articles in a retail store." The fact that a customer bought direct from the factory did not mean that the goods were cheaper. The normal channels of distribution, rather than being eliminated, were merely consolidated. The implications of "Direct to you at factory price" were "entirely fraudulent and misleading."[6] The author of the report felt that in order to endure, door-to-door selling must render a service, such as educating the consumer to new products.

The door-to-door industry today provides few real services to the consumer. The real advantages all accrue to the salesman or to the saleswoman. For 650,000 women—mostly Avon ladies—door-to-door selling provides a source of extra income.

For college students it provides a way of working their way through school. I interviewed the president of a boiler manufacturing company in Texas who sold pots and pans when he was a student. Besides earning good money, he felt that the experience in selling was excellent, whether it was pots and pans or industrial boilers. "Selling," he said, "is all the same." He looked for some flicker of interest when he gave his sales talk, and then stressed that subject. The pots and pans he sold were stainless steel, and the competition were aluminum sets, which were then very popular. He pitched the health advantages of stainless over aluminum, and one evening he noticed that the family seemed particularly interested in the vitamin retention of waterless cooking, and he settled down to work the theme. The father finally broke down in tears—he was fully convinced that they needed the cooking utensils for their daughter, who was in very poor health, but he knew he couldn't afford them. The salesman told me he felt terrible about it, but "You strike a nerve, and you work it hard."

For about 850,000 men, many without marketable skills, door-to-door selling provides a full-time job and a higher income than they might otherwise obtain.

Door-to-door salesmen emphasize that they offer the customer a chance to examine their merchandise and try it out right in the home—no need to contend with baby sitters, traffic, parking, and busy or disinterested store clerks. And, according to Mr. Lloyd Deilke, President of the National Association of Direct Selling Companies, "For many consumers the social aspect of direct selling has brightened their lives."

It is a pleasure to report that the most successful direct-selling companies are honest and reliable firms, but it is a regrettable fact that the direct-selling industry is plagued by companies whose salesmen prey largely upon the poor, the gullible, and the aged. Their favorite products are food freezers, vacuum cleaners, sewing machines, aluminum siding, fire and burglar alarms, correspondence courses, "get rich" schemes, franchises, chinchilla breeding stock, and encyclopedias.

Perhaps the most destructive character is the "customer peddler" who works the inner city, timing his visit at biweekly intervals, just behind the postman who carries the welfare and social-security checks. The peddler cashes the checks without charge (the bank charge $.10– $.20), a gesture that saves a trip to the bank for an elderly person or a mother, who may have a brood of young children.

The credit he extends, at exorbitant interest rates, is of importance, because local merchants are not supposed to open charge accounts for welfare recipients without the approval of the social worker. Such approval is difficult to obtain. David Caplovitz, in his study *The Poor Pay More*, concluded that the poor risks (i.e., the poor) are presented with two options: foregoing major purchases or being exploited. One recent example of slum peddling at its worst involved a New York company that grossed $3 million dollars a year selling burglar alarms. The alarms, worth about $30, according to the New Jersey Attorney General's office, were sold on a lease-purchase price of $550 and were supposed to be connected to the police department. The salesmen also told the buyers that the contracts were cancelable, when in fact they were not, and 2500 New York buyers who fell behind on payments were sued. The Consumer Affairs Department got a consent decree to force the company to refund some $125,000. The company has since declared bankruptcy, although it is believed to still be operating in New Jersey.

The "customer-peddler" is not only prevalent in the urban slums but thrives in the rural South. There, a motorized version of the wagon peddler tours the shanty towns, selling overpriced merchandise on easy, easy credit. One of the salesmen, who quit his route in disgust, said that the goods he sold were so overpriced that the first payment often covered their cost. As in the city, the people in the Carolina backwoods were grateful for the credit and seemed unaware that they were being overcharged, although the average markup was over 200 percent, and in some cases, much more. A framed picture of Dr. Martin Luther King, Jr., worth about $1.50, was sold for $19.50. The rural peddlers made between $200 and $300 a week.

Dishonest salesmen are not exclusively concerned with the poor. The middle class is hit largely by the "home improvement" salesman. The most famous of this genre are the Terrible Williamsons, a clan of about 2000 gyp artists who tour the country educating luckless citizens in the ways of "flim flam." "In a classic Williamson maneuver, a few of the men will drive up to a house in a tank truck. They have just resurfaced somebody's driveway, they say, and they would hate to waste their leftover blacktop. They offer to resurface the driveway for a bargain—and the homeowner accepts. Later, when the rain washes the 'gunk' off the driveway, the swindled homeowner realizes that the 'blacktop' was crankcase oil."[7] The Delaware Valley *News* (Frenchtown, New Jersey) reported a number of swindles by itinerant blacktoppers and lightning-rod peddlers in July of 1970. Were they Williamsons? Nobody knows. One was from Florida, and the rest were identified only as "out of state."

Very little is known about the clan, except that it is inbred, with names like Stewart, McDonald, and Reid,

as well as Williamson (descended from Robert Logan
Williamson, a Scottish emigrant who settled in Brooklyn
in the 1890s), and they bury their dead in Cincinnati,
which has the advantage, for this wandering tribe, of
being centrally located.

Some of the most expensive buying mistakes are
made by homeowners trying to save money. The home-
improvement industry is made up of a jumble of legiti-
mate contractors and builders along with some uncon-
scionable scoundrels. The National Better Business Bureau
has recorded more complaints about the home-improvement industry—arising from door-to-door sales—than from
any other single source. Homeowners lose between $500
million and $1 billion a year on frauds and gyps.[8]

There are several ways for the swindler-salesman to
find his mark. In some housing developments the telephone company can obtain an easement from a homeowner to install a telephone booth in front of his house.
For a fee, the homeowner lets the company use a corner
of his front lawn. One aluminum-siding company sent out
salesmen to look for telephone booths, reasoning that the
homeowner who allowed it to be put there was a
"mooch," i.e., someone out for something for nothing.
They rang the bell and made their pitch to the mooch,
or his wife: "Since you have such a lovely house, we
would like to feature it in a television commercial for
our aluminum siding. In exchange for letting us take a
few pictures and talk about your house on television, we
will put the siding on for cost." The quoted price is usually
about twice the going rate, but the mooch doesn't know
this, since he never really thought about aluminum siding
before. He figures he'd better grab this deal before they
offer it to someone else. He signs. Just to be sure the
mooch doesn't back out, the salesman "inspects" the
house with a crowbar, ripping off a board or two that
he says is rotten. He assures the homeowner (r-r-r-rip)
that it's a lucky thing all this is going to be covered

over (r-r-r-rip). It's called "spiking" a house. The next morning the aluminum siding is dumped onto the front lawn, by the telephone booth, and there it sits until the company gets around to installing it.

The amazing offer—or the fantastic bargain—is another hustle. An advertisement in a local newspaper promises a complete roofing job for $100. This time, the homeowner who calls for the salesman knows how much a roofing job costs, and he knows the $100 is *really* cheap. The salesman comes to see him, and the man signs an ironbound contract for the job. Then the salesman goes to work. "Did you see a sample of the kind of roof you just bought at the Home Show? No? Well, here is a sample for you to look at." It's horrible! The man doesn't want that wretched stuff on his roof, but he's already signed the contract. Now the salesman suggests an alternative. He has a better-grade roof which he will put on for $800. In which case he'll tear up the first contract.

The worst home-improvement racket thrived in Washington, D.C. The homeowner signed a contract at a price much higher than the salesman had quoted him. The work thus contracted for was, in many cases, never done. The contract was sold to a bank or a finance company—the holder in due course—who went to court to collect. Some people even lost their homes.

The deceptive door-to-door magazine salesman, although of a less serious nature, is another big source of complaints. Representative Fred Rooney (Democrat from Pennsylvania) wants legislation to regulate magazine salesmen, charging that a "substantial number" of the $150 million worth of subscriptions sold annually depend on deception.

The salesman's favorite theme is that he isn't selling anything, that you just won a contest and you are entitled to five years of these great magazines free. Naturally, you have to pay postage and handling, but this is only a few cents a week. The few cents a week—many of the magazines are *monthlies*—comes to over $100 for the contract period. After consumer complaints and the threat of legislation, four major magazine publishers drew up a code of ethics that would blacklist any magazine salesmen who violated it.

Later, in April of 1971, Time, Inc., agreed to a three-day grace period in which a new subscriber could cancel any magazines sold by a door-to-door salesman. The agreement was in response to a consent order from the Federal Trade Commission following complaints of "unfair and deceptive sales tactics."[9]

Encyclopedia salesmen are frequently the bad boys of the consumer movement. One door-to-door company ran afoul of the Consumer Affairs Department in New York when it offered to enroll customers in a nonprofit mother's club for $.89 a week for 297 weeks. Members received a "free" children's encyclopedia and other educational materials. The total contract added up to $264 for what the Department estimated was about $50 worth of books and materials. The "delivery" man who brought the books gave the customer a new contract to sign which called for payments of $11 a month.

In another action, the Department said that any state resident who had bought a World Book Encyclopedia from a door-to-door salesman on credit since September of 1970 could get a refund, because the publisher had failed to notify the buyers of the three-day "cooling-off" period called for in a new state law during which an order placed with a door-to-door salesman might be canceled.

The encyclopedia salesman is probably the most ubiquitous of the house-to-house callers, and one of the most successful. The Encyclopaedia Britannica advertises for salesman, offering a $1000-a-month written guarantee. The first year "potential" is, they say, $30,000–$45,000.

A favorite ploy used by many encyclopedia salesmen is the "survey" and the "opinion poll." They just want to show you the book. They also collect testimonials, and if you want to say something nice about the books and let them tell other people you own a set, they'll give you a special price. *Now* only.

One encyclopedia salesman worked out his own unique selling approach. He dressed like J. P. Morgan and drove a Mercedes into the nearest run-down neighborhood. The kids on the street immediately take notice, and before long they are crowding around the car. He strikes up a conversation and then asks around, "Son, is your mother home?"

Eventually he comes to little Billy. ("Little Billy" is a trade name for the sympathetic child. One vacuum-cleaner salesman used "little Billy" as his crippled son at home, who is waiting for the phone to ring to find out if Daddy sold enough vacuum cleaners to win him that little pony his heart is set on. As a last appeal, the salesman hands the near-customer the phone, with tears streaming down his face, and sobs, "Here, you tell little Billy he can't have that Pony.")

The dandy salesman follows his "little Billy" home and is introduced to Mama. The pitch is simple: Give little Billy a chance to make something of himself. The salesman tells of how he grew up in the slums, and how he read the encyclopedia by candlelight until he became a success. Shows her his car out in the street. Nice clothes. All the symbols. He leans heavily on the guilt. "Your son can be somebody for no more than you pay for . . . (cigarettes, beer, chewing gum, paper napkins, or whatever fits)." If all his pleadings fail to close the sale, he has one last trick, and he says it's successful one time out of four. There is usually a photograph of the child somewhere in the room, and he walks over and picks it up and says with infinite sorrow, "God Bless you, little Billy. I'm sorry I let you down."

A less imaginative but equally successful method of selling encyclopedias is to call on Puerto Rican families,

preferably those who barely speak English, and tell them
that the Department of Education requires them to have
a set.

An Illinois State Representative, Jack E. Walker,
arguing against legislation for a three-day cooling-off
period during which a customer could cancel a door-to-
door sales contract, said, "Our forefathers had to think
for themselves. Now, let the Puerto Ricans and these
other groups that complain about door-to-door sales think
for themselves."[10] Mr. Walker is evidently among those
who is nostalgic about fraud.

A similar law was proposed in the United States
Senate and hearings were held, the substance of which
supplied much of the research for this chapter. The bill,
S1599, died on the Senate Calendar, although many states
have passed a cooling-off law. At this writing, the Federal
Trade Commission is holding hearings on the proposed
regulation of door-to-door salesmen.

It seems odd that we should still have door-to-door
salesmen. I suppose it's no odder than the current preva-
lence of sidewalk peddlers now busily hawking umbrellas,
handbags, belts, wigs, scarves, and junk jewelry in mid-
town New York. There is something about the one-to-one
confrontation with a salesman that people want or need
or can't resist. It is perhaps the lure of the bargain,
founded on the belief that a single peddler can sell more
cheaply than a big store. While this is sometimes true,
it is worth remembering that the single peddler is
living off the profits of his meager stock, whereas the
big store can settle for a smaller profit. Whatever the
reason, neither common sense nor past experience seem
sufficient to break the spell.

The most interesting thing about the growing number
of street vendors is that, like those first peddlers of 1650,
they are mostly young people who are out to get started,
working around a system that seems to exclude them.
One young peddler told a reporter that she earned from

$60 to $90 a day, which is at least as good as those Yankee peddlers ever did.

The only positive value that door-to-door selling has in American society is that it is good summer work for students—good preparation for life and a fitting replacement for the newspaper route. From the salesman's point of view, it is the least desirable work, and from the consumer's point of view it is the most objectionable form of salesmanship. The salesman at the door is successful to the extent that he can impose himself on people who are too timid to tell him to go away, or who are entrapped by their own greed into the erroneous belief that the man who has appeared at their door is going to give them something free.

Nobody likes door-to-door selling, and nobody needs it, but we have it, and if present trends continue, we will have more.

Chapter Twelve

The Perfect Salesman

The small, neat wife of C. Arthur Kent smiled as he walked away, walking with a spring in his step down the flagstone path. She always had a smile for him as he left their small, neat colonial-split-ranch house on Sunday afternoons, even though his thirteen-week absences caused her an occasional pang. Lois Kent's smile was brave because a smile was part of her job. A wife was vitally important to the man in the field. But it must be said that she smiled too because her husband was such a fine, hard-working, good-looking man.

As she waved once at his retreating back, she turned and re-entered the house. She didn't want to watch the Plymouth station wagon pull away, and she looked around as if seeing her house for the first time. It *was*, in a sense, the first time, for they had moved in only the day before, into their fourth house in as many years. This was a nice one, better than the French Provincial Cape they had had before, and the Company had been good enough to send her ahead to find it. Then they had Mayflower come in, of course, and pack and wrap everything. The moving men did the whole job, swathing everything in sight—dishes, records, the hi-fi, the bar things, the bedding, one of the children. (Inadvertently, to be sure. It was Betsy, the quiet girl, but Art discovered that she was missing before the men got very far.) There was a great deal to pack because the house was filled with premiums earned by Art in sales contests.

At times, Lois thought that the Company did make a few too many demands on the family, perhaps . . . but then they always paid for the extras, like having the draperies shortened to fit the new windows. If the Company sometimes seemed to be a kind of rival for Art's time, affections, and energy, at least it was nice to know that his infidelities were committed with an old friend. Once again, Lois Kent smiled to herself.

Art Kent, on the other hand, never had to be told not to look back. He was feeling especially fit. His shirt, as always, was white; his tie, lively but not loud; his hair, freshly cut. His neck was freshly cut, too, but that was one of the hazards of trying out a new barber. He was wearing his favorite Glen Plaid, size 38 regular, headed for work in Territory 24, a man who was thirty-six years old and happy about it all. (He sometimes thought of himself, with a chuckle, as a perfect 38–24–36.)

As he bent to get into the green wagon, it struck him again that Sunday was a fine time of the week. A hearty breakfast first thing, church in the morning, a little drinkee before a good dinner, and then—off. Today, the slate was clean, the sky open, the road ahead clear, and every customer an old friend. Art's enthusiasm for his work ran deep, but never more freely than when setting off on Sunday afternoons. He looked out of the corner of his eye at the uncut lawn, saw the garage door hanging slackly from one of its hinges, and thought pleasantly of the motels and hotels somewhere beyond.

Before he drove away, he made a quick check of

the rear seat, making certain that his samples and order forms were in shape and that his itinerary was beside him. Because Art was a careful planner, and conscious of the value of time, everything was in place. He could only hope, with a slight smile, that those people he had written and phoned for appointments were having as good a weekend.

Plan? Perhaps he should have thought to blow a kiss at Lois. But no matter. A sound marriage, especially to a good kid like Lo, did not depend on one kiss more or less. He pressed down on the gas and dug out for the far country.

Maybe it wasn't really a far country—let's not romanticize everything, he thought—but he did feel that Territory 24, made up of southern West Virginia, western Maryland, the east-central regions of New Hampshire, and most of the Dakotas, except the major cities, was a wide world unto itself. It was full of rich, almost undeveloped Purchasing Power Potential. Certainly no other salesman of his acquaintance made quite the same set of varied stops. And he knew it like the palm of his hand. Well, the palm of his right hand, the east-central portion of his left, and his shoulder blades. (He didn't get to the Canadian border towns as often as he might. Bill Tincture was always on him about that.) He knew the best roads, the shortcuts, the rest stops, and the places where they gave traveler's discounts. He also knew that, as Tincture was always saying, the shortest distance between two customers is a straight line. Art's line *was* straight. He had a good product line, believed in it, and was, second only to enthusiastic, sincere about his work.

The next morning, after driving the first leg of his 1600-mile trip, Art decided to stop for breakfast at a favorite watering spot, The Forceps. It was near his first account, right across the street from a medical school, and this gave him a chance to drum up a little long-range business for the house. He liked to start out early, take time for a good breakfast, and, as he ate, study the new product literature that came crowding into his mailbox at home.

Entering the restaurant, he smiled at Perkins.

At first it had seemed odd that a waitress should be named Perkins—odd, that is, until he realized that Perkins was an unusual girl. The most distinctive thing about her, perhaps, was her mammoth bust, a great shelf of flesh underneath a tiny head. She had wonderful hips and really bad legs. The total effect was a sort of Fun House look that on some mornings was a trifle disconcerting. Still, Perkins had an unfailingly cheerful disposition to match the look. In fact, that was probably why Art liked her and liked The Forceps, crowded as it was; he, too, was pleasant and sociable, almost to a fault.

Though it could not be said that he was *too* sociable. He seldom went beyond a friendly good morning. He understood their motives, but he was an entirely different breed of man than the truck drivers who piled in there at all hours. Their trucks ranged outside like so many steel dinosaurs, they crowded the counters, downing their coffee and gobbling up the bad food with considerable racket, ogling Perkins' massive mantelpiece, shaking their heads, and smiling at her the whole time. They kept the place overly busy; unfortunately, they had learned long since that the best eating places are where salesmen stop to eat.

Perkins went by, bearing three slices of banana cream pie. Art stared. Then he brightened. He sensed the attractions of The Forceps' formidable waitress, but they were no problem. He was not only a dependable Company man, he was a dependable Lois man.

The Company was a warm concept in Art's mind, although he was never fooled. There was, after all, no such thing as *the* company. Any corporation is only a collection of men, all different. And Art was proud to be one of the field reps for Titan Pharmaceuticals. The "Titan" was presumptuous. They weren't actually the titans in their field. Fad-Globule were the big boys—in like Flynn, wheeling and dealing. No, Titan was not the biggest, but they were easily the best, Art believed, and they ranked just where they wanted to, in the middle range. Their annual sales volume was $388 million, and this year they were running nicely ahead, about 68 percent over last year.

Not that the heat was off. Volume was way up, but profits were down a hair. Art was, if he was anything, a profit-conscious salesman. In fact, thinking about Titan's situation caused him to erase the beginning of the call report he had started to make out while waiting for his coffee, rather than reaching for a new sheet. It was a silly error. Instead of writing his name at the top, he had written instead, in his clear, vigorous handwriting, the single word *money*.

Well, it couldn't be denied. Art was not only a lover of Lois, of home, of his job, and of the road—he liked money. Titan approved. They were forever urging him to make more, and they didn't seem to be embarrassed when one year he had finally said that soon he would *have* to make more, or else. They received this ultimatum in a good-natured, friendly, chaffing spirit, although he wondered whether the "greedy" rating on his biweekly Appraisal Sheet the following week had been the result of mentioning his plight. At any rate, Art could use more money—who couldn't?—and he would work to get it. This was the year. He didn't give a damn whether Lew Strichnine had made $30,000 last year and was over his quota by September . . . you couldn't rest on your oars. Not with two and a half kids (Lois, a good Art woman, was that way again), even with a decent income. Art made $15,000 a year gross, plus bonus and commission, and what with profit-sharing, plus the Titan Incentive Formula, contest prizes and other benefits, less expenses, he netted around $5200. Not a king's ransom exactly, Art thought, but maybe up until now he had been just a crown prince.

He laughed out loud. Perkins, passing again, lifted one thin eyebrow on the miniature face. "What's wit' chou?" she asked. She always covered up her unfailingly cheerful disposition with a flawless impersonation of Chesty Puller.

"Nothing, Perk, nothing," Art said, smiling.

After breakfast he put a tip beside the plate, pushed away the solidified, untouched eggs, swallowed the last drop of coffee, and stood up. He glanced a final time at Perkins, her vast, frozen, snowy white Northern Hemisphere topped by the curious little face like a grapefruit, shook his head, waved at her, and left.

Art's first call that morning was on Dr. Charles Phosphate, a crusty old character who had never written a prescription for a Titan drug in his life. He was always surly, often rude, and he usually had Art wait, along with the expectant mothers, the red-splotched children, and the broken-legged skiers, and then sent out word that he would not be able to see him. Phosphate often ran past Art in the waiting room, clutching his small black bag. It was, the nurse told Art, only a pose; he hadn't had a rush call in years.

But Art had him on the list. These objections could be overcome. If Art was anything, in addition to being a man of considerable enthusiasm, he was persistent. He'd get the old goat to write for Titan if he had to create a new illness. On one of the few occasions when he had managed to talk with Phosphate himself, Art put up with the usual guff and then merely remarked, quietly, "I only wish I had ten more customers like you, Doctor." This startled the old son-of-a-bitch for a moment.

"What did you say?" the doctor replied.

"I said, Doctor, that I only wish that I had ten customers like you."

"How can you say that?" Phosphate said. "I have a reputation with detail men for being an absolute son-of-a-bitch."

"Yes, that's true, Doctor," Art said evenly. "And you are. The trouble is, I've got forty or fifty more accounts like you; I only wish it were ten."

As he opened the door this morning, Art heard the bell ring in the office beyond. Good. No one in the waiting room. After a moment, a new nurse, an ash-blonde with a rather large face and tiny breasts, looked out at him. He gave her his card. "Oh, good morning, Mr. Titan," she said. "The doctor isn't—"

"Oh, yes he is," Art said. "I've got samples of Usurpine, a new item, and he doesn't get a sniff if I don't get in there."

The nurse's eyes widened, then narrowed. She knew Dr. Phosphate's interest—lust, in fact—in the detailers' free samples.

"All right," she said. "I'll see if he's—"

At that moment the door smashed open beside her and a wiry figure came hurtling past. Art could barely make out the craggy outlines of a white-maned head and the swinging black bag.

Just as the door slammed behind him, the nurse shouted, "Samples, Doctor!" For a moment, the only sound in the waiting room was the hissing of the steam radiator. It was close in the room, and Art stared at the woman fixedly. Her head was really immense and her bosom an intriguing miniature, a scale model, really, HO gauge. But he was a Lois man.

Then the outer door opened a crack and the beak of the doctor's proud, leonine head was visible.

"Samples?" he whispered.

The nurse nodded.

The shabby but somehow distinguished figure came back into the room. "Well," he said briskly, "let's have the next appointment."

"It's that nice young man from Titan Pharmaceuticals," she said. Art pretended to be looking at the magazine table. Like everything else in the room, it attested to the success of the doctor's practice, littered as it was with copies of *Show Business Illustrated*, *Flair*, *Collier's*, and a bound volume of *Liberty*. Beside it, a large plant was dying elaborately in a plastic pot.

"Yes," said the doctor, disappearing into his office. "Yes. Show him in."

Art Kent's next appointment was at Klein's. Klein Apothecaries, the leading account in the same town, had been, years ago, a drugstore; a dark cavern, lined with wooden and glass cases, with huge glass decanters in the dusty windows filled with mysterious red and green liquids, and a giant-size bottle of Coca-Cola. In the thirties, a son of the original owner took over and the place went straight downhill.

The next proprietor was a hustler, a man who ripped out the oak medicine closets and put in a soda fountain. The town was shocked at first, but the reaction turned into business. Then, with the death of that owner, *his* son took over and went too far. He put in tables and chairs and eliminated the space for compounding prescriptions. He stocked only the obvious staple drugs, and often substituted one for the other without checking with the attending physician. In addition to a slovenliness that amounted to criminal malpractice, he also put in a full line of toys and lisle hosiery. Business fell off, despite diversification, and when Art took over the territory, he had the good fortune to walk into new management.

The new Klein (his real name was Kerensky, but he kept the Klein for the sake of business) was, as Art described him, a druggist still wet behind his diploma.

But he had capital. He threw out the soda fountain and the hosiery, the magazine racks, and instead gave the whole place over to drugs. It was a store for people who needed modern medical miracles, and it was a beauty. There were oak closets lining the walls, and several glass-fronted cabinets, and in the window were several large decanters filled with colored liquids, and outside an old-fashioned sign reading, "Proprietaries and Ethical Drugs." A really progressive account. Art suggested that Klein-Kerensky look for one of those big display bottles of Coke —remember them? And he had helped him set up shop, seeing to it that certain racks, usable only for Titan patent products, were sunk into the concrete floor. Later, when the tile had set, Art wrote in his weekly sales analysis that Titan's future there was "built-in." This was repeated in the *Titan Co-Worker*, the Company house organ, and it earned a citation of merit in Art's service jacket in Personnel.

Klein was a small man, graying rapidly because of the pressures of small business (he was thinking of adding a soda fountain), but still full of energy. In that, he matched Art. Perhaps that was one of the reasons why they were such good friends. Art tried to be a friend to every customer. He liked all people. He loved some people. He was a person who needed people. Though he was unswervingly loyal to the Company, Art always let it be known that he was a customer's salesman, and was there more to render service, really, than to sell. Klein appreciated this, and friendship blossomed.

That morning, walking in, Art could see in Manuel Klein's face approval of the salesman's erect posture and his glowing good health. He stopped to finger a plastic ball filled with shampoo. It paid to show an interest in other kinds of merchandise, showed that you were interested in a man's entire business.

Even his voice, Art suspected, pleased Klein, because he kept it carefully modulated, speaking clearly and with

varying emphases. "Good morning, Mr. Klein," he said.
Courtesy was important, even with old friends.

"Kent," the small man said softly, his eyes watering.
Klein seemed to be, for just a brief moment, speechless.
Art warmed. Sometimes it was worth it to be enthusiastic,
honest, to keep your promises, to contribute ideas, to be
conscientious, and yet competitive. They shook hands.
(Art's grip was firm. Tincture, Titan's Director of Marketing, always said, "A firm handshake is the firm's best
representative.")

"WHERE THE HELL ARE MY ASPRINS?" Klein
shouted. His face went purple with rage.

Well, thought Art, back to business.

"Aspirin, Manny?" he asked, politely.

"Yes, my Ghadamn asprins," the man said. His grip
on Art's hand was enough to tear it loose from the wrist.

"Aspirin? Oh, you must mean *Whist*. We never refer
to it as aspirin alone. It's called Whist because it acts
faster in the lower digestive tract. Might take a little
longer getting down there . . ." he said, chuckling and
thinking of Whist's great bulk, "but it's up to nine times
as fast because—"

"Yes, yes, I know," Klein said, "because it's five times
as big." Art glowed. He put away the tear sheet of Titan's
current ad campaign.

"Well, where the hell *are* they?"

"Hey, *now,* just a minute . . . ," Art said. "Let's sit
down. I want to hear this out. You mean to say"—he
paused—"you mean to say, man, that those seven gross
of aspirins you ordered three weeks ago aren't here *yet?*"
His voice edged with incredulity and began to take on
a touch of Klein's accent.

"MONTHS!" Klein shrieked. "THREE MONTHS!
Not today yet. Not last month yet. Not the last time you
were here."

He sat down heavily. The rage passed. Klein wiped
a hand thick with the years of work and the morning's

grime across his lined forehead. "You sunning bitch," he said quietly. "You and that lousy mismanaged monopolistic company you work for. You—" He stopped. For the first time, it was too much to go on. Art reached across the little table and laid a hand on his shoulder. Lesson Seven: Let the customer's objections deflate themselves.

"Get'cher rotten hands off me," Klein said, his energy returning. "Look, Kent—Asprin. A-S-" He began to spell it out, abandoned the effort. "I can understand you don't get me the tranquilizers. Everybody's on tranquilizers. We're an untranquil country; we're gonna blow up in each other's face; I *understand* there should be a run on happy pills. *I* understand, *you* understand? But I have a clientele that only eats tranquil pills on holidays. The rest of the year they live on asprins. You understand? Asprin is my *bread!* If I'm a baker, asprin is my bread. Not my blueberry pies, not my pockerhouse rolls, not my blintzes—my absolute bread."

Art jumped to his feet. "Don't go on, Mr. Klein," he said. "What I am going to do is call—from here—I'm going to *place a long-distance call to Titan's main office* and I'm going to find out *what happened to your order.*"

Klein slumped wearily, then was instantly transformed into a wreath of smiles. A customer had entered. He stood up. As he left to attend her, he whispered to Art, smiling broadly: "Call collect, basstid. Collect."

Things worked perfectly. Art would simulate the call, bellow loudly, issue commands, with his back to Klein and the customer, and his hand pressing down on the hook. Art would mark the complaint up in triplicate on a Look Up sheet and fire it off that night.

He had called the plant often in the past, until the order came through to lay off. The phone bills, Tincture memo'd, "were about the size of the national debt. Unless you're in trouble, like trapped in a burning diner, *write,*

don't call. Any man who calls without real problems has
the cost of the call deducted from his Pension Fund."

Art made the "call" as realistic as possible.

After giving the number, he waited for a minute or
two, then said: "Hello—Titan? Gimme Tincture's office."

A pause. Then, loudly: "He is? Tincture's gone? Who
replaced him?"

Klein and the lady customer were watching. Kent
nodded. "Oh. He is? Fine, good man." He put his hand
over the mouthpiece, breathed confidentially at the
watching pair: "Tincture. Fired. They threw him out because the staple shipments got all balled up." He looked
back at the phone. "Okay, well . . . no, skip it. Just
wish what's-his-name luck for me. Kent. Territory 24.
That's right." He decided to make it completely authentic,
remembering the last time he had actually called. "No,
K-E-N-T. C. A. Kent. Yeah, that's it. Like the cigarettes.
Okay. Okay, 'bye." He put everything into it. Art was
part actor, and he was, if nothing else, enthusiastic about
everything he did.

"Fine," Klein said, waving a hand at him. "Okay,
you did your best."

"All right to look through the prescription file?"

Klein stared at him for a second, then gave the weary
wave again.

"Thanks, Manny," Art said. "I wish I had ten customers like you."

——, he thought, walking to the back room where
Klein kept the precious, indecipherable white slips from
the neighborhood doctors, to see who was writing for
his stuff.

These episodes from the life of a traveling man are
almost as ridiculous as some sales administrators' ideas
of life on the road. C. A. Kent—his first name is Clark,
of course—is a composite, somewhat tilted, of the prevailing ideas about the ideal salesman. He is a small

Superman. He is likable, aggressive, resourceful, independent, loyal, enterprising, dutiful, energetic, ambitious but restrained, a hideous and impossible wax dummy.

But the qualities he exhibits are all in constant demand, and if we are to take marketing management seriously, one is expected to find these qualities in the right measure within the same man. Which is more fanciful—the fable or the fact that a large part of the nation's sales time is spent looking for, or at least talking about, men like Clark Kent?

Chapter Thirteen

The Personality of the Salesman

There have been many attempts over the years to unravel the personality of the salesman, and most of the interest has been motivated by the employer's desire to know a good salesman when he sees one.

Are there personality traits common to all salesmen? Can a test be devised to select potential salesmen from a random group of applicants? The answers to those questions could save time and money on salesmen who fail when they are sent out on their own.

No approach to the problem has been ruled out. At one time phrenology was seriously suggested as the answer. A sales manager, addressing the Salesman's Club of Duluth back in 1916, said that when he hired a salesman he wanted "a man whose face is broad between the eyes, with a sales nose . . ."[1] One company measured the size of each applicant's head and hired him if it was big enough, reasoning that because a salesman used his head, it should be rather large.

Another company got a photograph and signature

from each applicant and combined phrenology with hand-writing analysis.

The users of these various methods were perfectly satisfied with the results, a fact that should be borne in mind when listening to recommendations for tests in use today.

Professor H. L. Hollingsworth of Columbia University was one of the first researchers to apply the scientific method to the mystical process of divining the presence of sales talent. He first directed his attention to the sales manager's interview with the sales applicant. The interview was the usual way of evaluating personality in those prescientific days, and was based on the manager's intuition and prejudices, reinforced with some small but crucial test.

The applicant, for example, might be left standing before the manager's desk for some time while he—the manager—continued to work, ignoring his visitor. Finally, the manager would look up and say, "Sit down. Take off your coat." There was neither chair nor coatrack in the room, and if the applicant perceived the insult and stormed out, the manager ran him down and offered him a job.

Professor Hollingsworth followed the careers of fifty salesmen who were interviewed by twelve sales managers. All the applicants were hired and given a territory to cover. After they had been on the road long enough to establish a sales record, Hollingworth examined the rating given them by various sales managers during the interviews and compared it with the salesman's actual performance on the job. He found the correlation so poor that he concluded the manager's opinion could be relied upon to be wrong.

He was thus convinced that the sales manager's interview, while it did show a response to sales talent when taken as an average, was a poor way to select salesmen. He proposed instead the empirical method, "based purely on facts, and does not make assumptions."[2]

He prepared a test for certain abilities such as color naming, number checking, letter substitution, and verbal skill. The test results of experienced and successful salesmen were then to be used as a profile for hiring. This is essentially the way salesmen are tested today, although different tests are used.

The use of psychological tests to select salesmen was not very common until the Second World War. After the war, the use of tests rose sharply. According to a recent survey,[3] large companies are more dedicated to testing than small companies. The large companies had been in business over forty years and were expanding their sales staffs. Their salesmen called on buyers from a wide range of companies, while salesmen from nontesting companies tended to call on industrial companies only.

Companies that used tests were found to have less turnover of salesmen than companies that did not use tests. However, among the nontesting companies there were more with no turnover, a paradox explained by the fact that a high turnover rate is the chief motivation for using testing. Companies with little or no turnover are less likely to start using tests. Most sales executives, in a survey by Schwartz, felt that the wife had a strong influence on the "voluntary termination" of the salesman. Almost all felt that her influence was "considerable" or "very considerable." Their solution was "to develop enthusiasm in the salesman's wife."[4]

One of the first significant applications of sales testing was in 1936. Tremco, a manufacturer of maintenance supplies, was concerned about its high turnover rate, caused largely by the fact that many salesmen were unable to sell enough maintenance supplies to earn a reasonable commission. It must have occurred to them that the rate of commission might have been too low and that the Depression had something to do with poor sales volume, but the fact that some of the salesmen were able to bring in enough business to live on was proof that all the salesmen should be able to. Territories were considered to be of equal potential, which was probably unreasonable. Lack of a reliable standard of comparison makes it difficult to differentiate between the many factors that influence a salesman's volume, not the least of which are a few big customers who need the product.

Tremco hired Dr. O. A. Ohman, a psychologist, to have a look at their business operations. Dr. Ohman studied the sales and personal records of Tremco salesmen for the previous twelve years, and found a number of factors that correlated with high sales volume.

The successful Tremco salesman was under forty years of age at the time he was hired. The poorest salesmen were between 40 and 44.

The successful salesman was tall, married, had one child (more than three was unfavorable), had $5000 or more in life insurance, was in debt, and belonged to no more than two clubs. Applicants with no debts or more than $500 in the bank did less well as salesmen.

The successful salesman completed whatever educational level he began. Those who completed the eighth grade, high school, or college fared about the same, but those who interrupted their education and failed to complete any of these formal educational levels were less successful as salesmen. It was better to have finished high school than to have dropped out of college.

The successful salesman was with the company ten years. The less successful salesman either left quickly or hung on for more than ten years. Some previous experience in building maintenance was favorable, but the number of years was not significant. Ten years of other work experience was optimum.

The best Tremco salesmen earned $200 to $250 a month on their previous job. The less successful salesmen often earned more on their previous job, between $250 and $300 a month.

Men who were employed when they were interviewed by Tremco were the best risks to succeed, followed by those who had lost their jobs through no fault of their own. Those who were fired or left because of friction were the poorest risks. The longer a man was out of work, the poorer were his chances of succeeding as a Tremco salesman.[5]

While these findings can lead to some interesting speculations, Dr. Ohman cautioned that the meaning of his data was completely unknown. The empirical does not suppose. It is difficult to determine if any of these factors have significance today, even within the same company.

A. J. Snow, a psychologist who studied the personality of the salesman, concluded that the salesman is credulous, that he is "an easy and ready believer." This trait "is a factor of social intelligence . . . of adaptability, of getting along with Tom, Dick and Harry in the various genial and trying situations of life. The salesman swallows rumors wholesale; he has his superstitions about Pullmans, samples, buyers, signs and omens. Credulousness also is responsible for making him open to conviction, while, on the other hand, he is a veritable armory of prejudices and commitments. What is his opinion about the next war, the state of crops, or fundamentalism? It is the opinion of the last man of force and personality . . . that he happens to have talked to at any length . . . To use an everyday figure of speech, the social intelligence of the salesman enables him to land like a cat on his four paws no matter where or how you throw him." Snow's book, *Psychology in Personal Selling*, was published in 1926, but no one has since added a gullibility factor to the salesman's personality test.

A more universal picture of the salesman was drawn in 1938 from the Bernreuter Personality Inventory. The salesman was found to be neither moody nor subject to worry. He was self-confident and self-sufficient, aggressive and willing to assume responsibility. He was social, had little tendency to talk about himself, was free from self-consciousness, and was not resentful of criticism or discipline.[6] Personality and interest in selling were considered predictive factors in hiring salesmen.[7]

There has been little that has been innovative in the study or practice of the hiring of salesmen. I recently talked to Dr. Arthur A. Witkin, president of the Sales Aptitude Testing Company, to find out what he looked for in a salesman. According to Dr. Witkin, the salesman is in the ninety-third percentile in verbal intelligence, ninety-second percentile in emotional stamina, and the eighty-seventh percentile in forcefulness. Dr. Witkin administers a long series of tests and interviews to probe for these basic qualities. Can he really pick out the promising salesman? "We can raise the batting average of the company doing the hiring," he said, declining to be more specific.

In his study of the use of psychological testing, Dr. Goldwag[8] quoted a sales executive who used the same batting-average metaphor to describe his experience with testing applicants. Since hiring the wrong man can cost up to $50,000—to use an estimate of the New York Sales Executives Club—the fee for a test would seem to be a good investment. The attitude is that while tests don't promise much, they don't cost much either.

The Bell System made an attempt to find a new way to hire "communications consultants," as they prefer to call their salesmen. They set up an Assessment Center in Cleveland, staffed by a director and six sales managers who had received three weeks' training in assessing prospective salesmen (assessees) for twenty qualities, which included "resistance to premature judgment, oral presentation, oral defense, behavior flexibility, and persistence."[9]

Men applying for sales work were sent to the Center

and given two days of interviews, tests, and group-participation projects such as leaderless discussions and peer ratings. The assessments were not revealed, and all of the men were hired. Later on, the assessments were compared with the reviews of the new salesmen by company supervisors after the men had been on the job. The accuracy of the assessments was not impressive, but the men who had conceived of the Center concluded that it was "a valuable aid."

Another new approach to the problem was devised by David Mayer and Herbert M. Greenberg. Their article in the *Harvard Business Review*[10] is still bringing industrial psychologists to boil faster than a Meker burner. Dr. Witkin rose straight out of his chair when I mentioned the article and called it "a hoax and a fraud." During a later interview, Dr. Greenberg dismissed Dr. Witkin's personality percentiles as "blatant nonsense."

Previous tests for salesmen have failed, Mayer and Greenberg said, because:

1) Tests have been looking for "interest" rather than ability. Because a man wants to sell doesn't mean he can. There are people more interested in baseball than Willie Mays and who can't play nearly as well.

2) Tests are fakable. Applicants answer the questions to get a job, not to be truthful.

3) Tests favor group conformity, not individual creativity.

4) Tests have tried to isolate fractional traits rather than to reveal the whole dynamics of the man. "Long before he comes to know the product, mostly during his childhood and growing-up experience, the future successful salesman is developing the human qualities essential for selling."

Those basic qualities, essential to the personality of the salesman, are empathy and ego drive. In 1952, Tobolski and Kerr noticed that little research had been done on empathy and its relation to sales ability, which seemed to them "a remarkable historical oversight by psychologists."[11] They gave a fifteen-minute Empathy Test to a group of Chicago new-car salesmen and found that the test scores were significant predictors of sales success. (The tests completely failed on used-car salesmen, which is probably more of a comment on those particular salesmen than on the test.)

According to Dr. Greenberg, empathy is like the heat-seeking missile that senses warmth and zeroes in—an unpleasant, but descriptive, analogy.

Ego drive is what makes the salesman want to sell in a personal way. "His self-picture improves dramatically by virtue of conquest, diminishes with failure. Since he must fail more often than he will succeed, the failure must act as a trigger." A man with an ordinary ego would quickly become discouraged in a situation that rouses the salesman to action. (In a study of self-imagery, Howton and Rosenberg discussed the difficulty the salesman has in coping with such conflicting demands. "The man who is expected to 'roll with the punches' while developing 'sensitivity' runs with the risk of losing his footing."[12])

Mayer and Greenberg devised a test for measuring empathy and ego drive that they claim is 89 percent accurate in picking surefooted salesmen from the stumbling herd.

I took the test twice. The first time I tried to slant my answers so that I would appear to be the embodiment of the kind of salesman always in demand in the want ads—self-starting, alert, aggressive, and willing to work. I reasoned that most men taking the test would respond as I had, in that they would answer in such a way as to satisfy the tester and the employer he represented.

The second time I took the test, I was entirely negative about the salesman's job and I was severely honest, overly critical in fact, about personal qualifications. It was Dr. Greenberg's contention that it was impossible to fake the test. Even if you distorted the answers, the way you distorted them would give you away.

Both times, I was recommended as a salesman. I cannot testify to the accuracy of that judgment, having never been a salesman, but it was interesting that I scored lowest the first time, when I had tried to appear to be a potential supersalesman. Dr. Greenberg explained that the first time I took the test I appeared to be over-aggressive and lacking in empathy. My exaggerations had been interpreted as a sign of insensitivity—more the bull-dozer than the heat-seeking missile. The second time I took the test, I did not attempt to portray myself as quite so energetic and enthusiastic. Consequently, I got a better rating, since my empathy and ego drive were more in balance.

Dr. Greenberg has applied his ideas about ego and empathy to sales training, using the test to find the salesman's strengths and weaknessess. The "impulsive, driven salesman" needs different training from the sales-man with a milder ego drive who is able to relate to the customer, but never gets around to asking for the order.

A frequent complaint about tests for salesmen is that they do not measure the applicant's *desire* to sell, and that tests are more likely to find reasons why an applicant should not be hired than to find good potential salesmen.

Tests are frequently wrong, and employers are warned against relying on test results rather than on their own judgment. While there are compelling economic reasons for testing salesmen, it is still a primitive art. At the Assessment Center mentioned earlier, for example, almost half of the men found "unacceptable" by the assessors did well on the job. Had the recommendations of the Assessment Center been followed, these men would have received an intensive evaluation and then been told that they had failed—a shattering experience in itself, and one of which the men who designed the test seemed totally unaware. The testers, in the process of raising their batting averages, are unconcerned with their strike-outs.

In examining the criteria of the tests, there are a number of disputed points. Dr. Witkin says the salesman is in the ninety-third percentile of intelligence—that is, as compared with the man on the street. Ronald Cloyd,[13] in an examination of business-machine salesmen, found that there was no correlation between either intelligence or education—above a certain minimum—and success as a salesman.

In order to evaluate the results of a test for sales ability, it is necessary to establish some way of measuring a salesman's performance. W. A. Tonning[14] made a study of this subject and found that, while evaluation was desirable, it was very difficult to do. Because of the many variables that affect a sale—economic conditions, lack of uniformity of customers, and other outside influences—a simple reading of the salesman's dollar volume is not always a reliable indicator of his ability.

Clement Nouri[15] attempted to evaluate how much effect the saleman's personal efforts had on sales volume. He found that the customer considered quality, delivery, and price as the most important considerations. The effectiveness of the salesman was rated as the tenth most important consideration. The salesman rated his own effectiveness as the third most important factor in making the sale. Neither the customer nor the salesman felt that the salesman was the most important factor in making the sale.

When the customers were asked to rate the salesmen according to personal characteristics and effectiveness, the salesmen rated the highest also had the biggest volume of business. There was also a high correlation between the number of sales calls and the volume of business. Obviously, the salesman's personality had an affect on sales volume, although Nouri was unable to measure it, and the customer and the salesman were unable to agree on its substantial presence. It is asking too much of coincidence to believe that the customer's favorite salesman consistently had the best product, the best delivery, and the best price.

The salesman is important to the sale, even in the supposedly cut-and-dried manner of industrial buying, but without being able to accurately evaluate a salesman's performance, it is impossible to evaluate an empirical test.

The "psychological tests" most widely used for testing sales ability are tests for intelligence, interest, personality and temperament, aptitude and achievement. These tests are inclined to produce an external, empirical view of the salesman, leaving untouched the more elusive and intriguing components of the salesman's personality, such as his values and imagery.

Howton and Rosenberg[16] interviewed sixty-six salesmen, "nearly all 'outside' men" from the New York area and in the upper-middle income bracket. They found that the salesman's self-image is a delicately balanced mechanism that allows him to function in the dual role of social hero and villain. "The composite view is that while selling is not a humiliating occupation, the salesman . . . can't help but feel humiliated if he has any sensitivity.

"The *occupation* is not humiliating but the *work* sometimes is. This interesting dichotomy makes it possible to (a) accept as one's proper due whatever respect is offered and (b) neutralize the wounding effect of rebuffs by claiming credit for being able to take it."

The salesman stresses the professional aspects of selling—training, product knowledge—but "he clings to the mystique of the drummer, the magic of personality, the inexplicable 'sixth sense of merchandising.' . . . The salesman's ideological strategy, in brief, is to seek to garner the best from both worlds: the aura of the professional man without the encumbrances, the aura of the drummer without the loss of respect."

Despite the fact that money was only occasionally mentioned by the salesman, the authors suspected that "striking it rich is what he is secretly set on."

While there have been many attempts to exploit the salesman's apparent need for recognition with prizes and games, many employers remain convinced that salesmen are consumed with thoughts of money. The sales manager of a pumping-equipment company, for example, said he wanted salesmen who were "selfish and money-hungry. . . . We want an acquisitive man who wants to make a pile of money and will work like a horse to get it, who cares more about money than about security, prestige or social responsibility." His ideal salesman was impatient, intelligent, and "doesn't really care whether people like him or not."[17]

This resonates with a study by Kirchner and Dunnette, who found that successful salesmen think of themselves as "successful, persistent, confident, opportunistic, persuasive, and ambitious." Less successful salesmen see themselves as "contented, handy, unselfish, leisurely, imaginative, tactful . . ."[18]

D. A. Rodgers found that salesmen were primarily interested "in the tangible and material and [had] a willingness to compromise readily on values in order to 'fit-in.'" He also found a "manipulative superficiality of values with people that conceals a basic mistrust of others and a lack of real concern for them behind a façade of friendly closeness."[19]

Dr. Greenberg expressed a somewhat similar view about the salesman who travels extensively: He is likely to be immature, since his choice of work precludes the building of close relationships, and even seems to be designed to avoid them.

The salesman depicted in test profiles is often a compilation of virtues and superlatives that ignores these

negative qualities essential to the salesman for his survival. One of the most destructive forces acting on the
salesman's personality was noted forty years ago by
Stuart Chase, and is virtually ignored by tests.

Chase was a critic of the ethical values of overselling, which, in his opinion, intruded into every facet
of the salesman's personality. He wrote, in opposition to
the growth of high-pressure salesmanship, that we were
losing our ability to "build friendships on the basis of
love and affection, rather than on the basis of what one
can get out of it. . . . 'Sell thyself' rather than 'know thyself' is the categorical imperative of the age."[20]

Many essays have been written since then on the
degree to which a man's self-esteem is influenced by
his success or failure to sell himself in the job market.
The salesman encounters such situations much more frequently than does the general population. In fact, he
encounters it daily, if not hourly. Selling oneself now
bears the more respectable title of self-alienation, "the
process whereby the seller 'sells' his own personality."
Sociologists maintain that "the most repellent aspect of
self-alienation lies in the fact that sellers themselves are
unaware of prostituting their personalities." It is the
leading occupational disease of salesmen today, and is
reflected in the salesman's frequent reiteration: "You got
to sell yourself."

The salesman has often accepted his accommodat-
ing role quite cheerfully. Albert Wright, a salesman who
traveled around the world before the First World War,
recounted his experiences among the strictly religious
Boers. "I tried to adapt myself to the ways of the Boer
people by doing as they did. When they prayed, I prayed
with them. When they laughed, I laughed too. And when
they cried, I tried to do likewise. I had so much coffee to
drink that at first it made me ill. And having to pray so
often wore my trousers out at the knees."

Marshall[21] argues that as mass production has tended

to render products more and more alike, the salesman
has had to rely increasingly on his own personality to
make the difference in the buyer's mind, an opposite
viewpoint from those who feel that modern salesmanship is above "personality" selling.

If these descriptions and their connotations of greed
and moral depletion sound familiar, it is because they
are also the epitaphs used by critics of the American
character in general. When Sinclair Lewis said that the
coroner's verdict at America's inquest will read "Killed
by Salesmanship," he referred to the fact that the salesman's personality is by no means limited to salesmen.

Almost certainly, psychological testing in the future
will be supplemented by personal information available in centralized computer banks. Dr. Witkin told an
interviewer: "We'll know, for instance, if an applicant
ever stole two dollars' worth of fishing cord when he
was a kid. Of course, something like this shouldn't bar
him from employment. But it's not difficult to understand why we should dredge up this fact and other
pertinent information (from religion to sexual esca-
pades), because we want to know as much as possible
about this man. . . . We cannot know in advance what
information will be most significant and critical in making that evaluation."[22]

Without going into the horrors of the future com-
puterization of one's life history, it is enough to point
out here that the test results would undoubtedly be fed
back into the computer, thus adding the machine's reputation for factual accuracy to the already overvalued
psychological appraisals.

Chapter Fourteen

The Cheerleaders

Having spent enormous sums of money locating, testing, and hiring the salesman—all done as scientifically as possible—sales managers then proceed on the metaphysical notion that selling is an act of will which requires that the salesman be enthusiastic. Getting the salesman excited about himself and his product is considered a valid way of building up his confidence to withstand the assaults and rejections routinely sustained in the daily course of selling. A salesman covering his territory has a lonely job—it has been said many times. He travels by himself, and most of the people he calls on will, in effect, rebuff him by not buying what he is selling. Perhaps because of the emotional involvement inherent in the buying act, a potential buyer who rejects a salesman's proposal often feels free to reject, and sometimes eject, the salesman. (Salesmen and public-relations men seem to be expected to absorb the frustrations of the people they deal with.)

His social life on the road, his reputation for dalliance notwithstanding, is usually limited to entertaining buyers. This ritual all-male courtship is typified by overeat ing and overdrinking, an experience the salesman will retain in his head and stomach more than in his heart.

By the time he returns to the home office, his spiritual fires need rekindling. Awaiting him there, will be a kind of cheering section, ready to comfort him with speeches, prizes, contests, and various other "incentive builders."

That cheering section has become a serious business over the years. Its invention, and a good deal of its refinement, is credited to John Patterson. Others were quick to admire and imitate the Cash. Morris and Company spent $50,000 on district sales conventions in 1917. Salesmen were invited to the conventions by a letter from the company president to allay the salesman's suspicion that he was being set up for a lecture by the sales manager.

In 1925, the Hoover Vacuum Cleaner Company brought its salesmen from the United States, Canada, England, Denmark, Holland, Sweden, and Switzerland for a sales convention which included a trip through the factory, a parade, a sports tournament, and a vaudeville night. In the parade there was a "prehistoric monster" (representing germs in dirt) that snorted and spouted dust. Another float carried a group of Minute Men and a large sign, "1775–The Minute Men Started To Clean Up: 1925–Hoover Men Continue It." No one perceived this as a criticism of the American Revolution.

The Ingersoll Company devised the system of splitting the business portions of conventions into a series of small conferences. Large meetings that experimented in corporate democracy sometimes got bogged down when one long-winded salesman after another seized the floor. The chairman countered by cutting them off with, "Put it in the suggestion box." The purpose of the meetings, after all, was "largely to send the salesman away feeling good. . . ."[1]

The bullring was a popular way to give the salesmen a chance to get their gripes off their chests. A company executive would seat himself before the salesmen, and they were encouraged to freely express their complaints and criticisms.

Having discharged the ill feelings, the second stage of the sales meeting was to educate and enthuse. Slide shows and movies were favorites for education, but more dynamic methods were employed for enthusiasm.

The Liberty Loan Company used cheer leaders at their sales meetings. The results greatly impressed W. C. Standish, a district sales manager for the United States Rubber Company: "At the Liberty Loan meetings it was highly essential that the men be fired with enthusiasm, so a chap who at one time had been a student at the University of Michigan mounted the platform, and every time a captain reported subscriptions amounting to $50,000 or over, the cheerleader called for the old University of Michigan college yell: 'Yea, Smith. Yea, Smith, Fight 'Em, Fight 'Em,'" etc. The idea caught on and was used at other conventions, with the added refinement of having each sales district have its own fight song, accompanied, in some cases, by their own "Jass [sic] bands."[2]

The football spirit was further evoked by fight songs and speeches resembling a coach's half-time harangues in the locker room. Knute Rockne made a sideline career out of giving talks to groups of salesmen, using "the Rockne voice and the Rockne manner of speaking for the purpose of dominating and inspiring"[3] the salesmen. He was about to accept a position as sales manager for an automobile company at the time of his death. Coaches and football players have been popular speakers at gatherings of salesmen since then, joined lately by golf players and astronauts. The connection between these various activities and salesmanship is not readily apparent, beyond their entertainment value.

No convention was without a song book. The United States Tire Company salesmen sang:

Royal Cord Tires are very swell.
They ride so well and wear so swell,
Your car is always handy.
Royal Cord Tires, Ha, Ha, Ha,
Royal Cord Tires, are dandy.
Royal Cord Tires, Ha, Ha, Ha.
They make your car ride dandy.

And at American Multigraph, they sang:

We love the Multy,
The bully, bully Multy,
It's as fine as the finest thing we know,
It's built to last forever,
And to boost it's our endeavor,
So that's the reason why we grow.

The most famous company fight songs were those of
IBM. "Hail to the IBM" was written in 1938 by Fred W.
Tappe, an IBM employee, and the music was contributed
by the composer Vittorio Giannini. The same team later
wrote "March on with IBM." And at every convention
IBMers sang the "rally" song, "Ever Onward":

There's a thrill in store for all,
For we're about to toast
The corporation known in every land.
We're here to cheer each pioneer
And also proudly boast
Of that "man of men," our friend and
    guiding hand.
The name of T. J. Watson means a courage none
    can stem.
And we feel honored to be here to toast the
    IBM.

It's hard to imagine how anyone sang those lyrics,
but thousands did over the years.
Since those early cornball days, a sizable industry

has evolved to educate and enthuse salesmen. Experts and professionals are called in to help. Consultants in the new science of group dynamics command a fee of about $500 a day, and one top meeting consultant gets $1500 for a day and a half of his council. I know one meeting consultant who charged a client $1600 for a program that took him only four hours to prepare.

Mr. Robert Letwin, editor of *Sales Meetings* magazine (circulation: 50,000), said that according to their research, the average national sales meeting costs $85.77 per day, per man. The average national sales meeting lasts 3.6 days and is attended by 160 people. If you multiply that out, as I did, you'll find it comes to just under $50,000. If you add up all the money spent on all the 287,000 district, regional, and national sales meetings held each year, as Mr. Letwin's researchers did, you might be surprised to find that it comes to $3.9 billion a year.

A Dartnell survey reported that in 1969, the average sales executive attends 20 meetings, workshops, seminars, and conventions a year, and conducts about 10. The record for one executive was 250.

Salesmen are beginning to attend sales meetings by telephone. TeleSession, a New York Company, uses special electronic equipment to set up nationwide telephone hookups to enable the salesmen to all talk together at a fraction of the cost of the simplest face to face meeting. Entire conventions can now be held by telephone. A salesman can dial into any of the group discussions he finds interesting and he can hang up on any he finds boring.

Most of the time and money spent on sales meetings is, in Mr. Letwin's opinion, wasted. No specific goals are set for what is to be accomplished by the meeting, and, of course, there is no way to evaluate the success of the meeting other than noting whether or not that everybody had a good time or enjoyed the speakers. The meeting becomes a ritual that the salesman accepts, some-what reluctantly, as being a nonproductive but required part of his job. His attitude is sensed by management, which responds by enlisting the services of an outside firm to liven up the meeting and keep the salesmen awake, hence the "dog and pony show," as dressed-up sales meetings are called. Organizations like Charisma Group, Inc. specialize in the "multimedia" show, which usually consists of a large number of Kodak Carousel projectors shining on a large screen, with maybe an actor employed as an M.C.

In many cases, the meeting is the message. Charisma Group did a sales-meeting show for IBM on the theme "What is the measure of a man?", and the M.C. wore a white suit decorated with a large tape measure. In this case the meeting, held for the Office Products Division, was a reward in itself, since it was attended only by those salesmen who had fulfilled their quotas for the year. The theme of these meetings is usually designed to enhance the self-esteem of the salesman either with as-suring topics such as "Professionalism" or "thoughtful" approaches on "Can Man Control His Destiny?" The company's message buried beneath these lofty sentiments, is often surprising. IBM, in this case, was concerned about employee turnover and wanted to assure the salesmen that IBM was concerned with their mortal soul and was, therefore, a good company to work for.

Such corporate pontificating is likely to strike some salesman as humorous, an impression he expresses at his own peril. At an IBM sales meeting, in the Data Proc-essing Division, one salesman who found mirth in the solemn proceedings laughed out loud and was fired on the spot. I have the story on good authority, albeit sec-ondhand.

Aside from the "reward" meeting, there are four basic reasons for holding a sales meeting: to transmit information; to give special training; to change attitudes; and to change the behavior of salesmen.

The hoopla that accompanies the achievement of these sober goals is not confined to those early-morning gatherings of vacuum-cleaner salesmen. The circulation manager of the Dow Jones Company, publisher of the *Wall Street Journal,* recently called together his eighty circulation salesmen and issued them white paper jump-suits to wear at the sales meeting. When they rustled into the meeting room they were treated to a light-and-sound show and a film of a moon landing. The circulation manager greeted them from a mock-up of a space capsule. The idea was to generate enthusiasm and "just make them feel good about things." One of the salesmen was quoted as saying: "I felt kind of goofy, especially when I walked through the lobby. It struck me as being a little silly for grown men to be acting like that."[4]

I met a sales manager once who presided over the sales force of a drug manufacturer. His men called on doctors and druggists, some in the city and some out in remote towns beyond the big snowbanks. It was cruel work. Calling on doctors is generally regarded as tough business, largely because doctors hate salesmen but love free samples.

When the manager visited the branches to urge his men on, he used his favorite act, if there were enough men on the staff who hadn't seen it. Turnover in that discouraging trade was sufficient to provide a constant supply of fresh faces. He would assemble them in a meeting room and yell nearly at the top of his voice: "You got to go after the customer. You got to get the drop on him!" Here he would pull out a couple of six-shooters and fire them off. "And you got to snow him!" Whereupon he would shower his awestruck charges with white confetti. I never had a chance to talk to any of the salesmen to get their impression of the act.

A sales manager I heard about would end a meeting

by telling his men to pick up their chairs and look beneath the seats. There they would find a ten-dollar bill taped to the bottom. His parting line was that if they got off their tails they could make some money.

Few sales managers consider such performances an adequate stimulus for their salesmen to break down the doors on their way out to break their quotas. But for all the sophistication modern business pretends to, life in some sales departments is not alien to such theatrics.

Another device to get salesmen to sell harder is the contest. The sales contest, like the sales meeting, is big business. Like other Patterson contributions to American salesmanship, the sales contest became a regular event in many companies. In 1927, the Eureka vacuum cleaner company was using sales contests to pick up volume during the lull that normally occurred after Christmas. The contest prizes offered by various companies ranged from straw hats to diamond fobs and automobiles.

Bob Blashek, Executive Vice-president of D. L. Blair & Company (leaders in the contest field), says no one really knows the total dollar value of the contest industry today. A free travel vacation is a favorite prize. "Incentive travel" is estimated to be worth $150,000,000 a year, and the "total incentive business" is estimated at twice that.

The reason contests are popular has to do with the psychology of the salesman and the nature of money and business. Sales managers like to see their salesmen with that hungry, feverish look. After a salesman has had a pretty good year, he tends to relax and behave in a manner that the outside world would consider normal and the sales manager considers lethargic. Motivational psychologists suggest that money is the most expensive motivational tool around. Dr. Lowen equates money with power and suggests that some people are unable to stand too much of it.[5] The level at which a salesman's pace slackens differs with the individual and with expectation.

Historically, salesmen have always been above-average earners, but they have rarely made big money. A man who remained a salesman throughout his business career had, with rare exceptions, decided not to be a rich man.

A manager who wishes to put on a hard sales drive has a problem if his salesmen have already had a good year. Further expenditure of money in the form of higher commissions or cash bonuses has proportionately less attraction to the salesman to greatly increase his efforts. The manager always has the option of firing his sales staff, and this has been done more than once, but it is a poor solution since the same problem will arise again.

In most companies the salesman's quota and the size of his territory are periodically adjusted to satisfy management's estimation of what their share of the market ought to be and to satisfy the salesman's estimation of what his income ought to be. Any short-term additional goals set during the year may be rewarded with prizes instead of cash.

The argument for prizes in lieu of money holds that extra cash tends to be absorbed into the family budget, and the salesman never experiences any real pleasure if he wins a sales bonus. The extra effort required to win a sales contest usually means that the salesman will be away from home more often. If his wife views this as just "working late," she is likely to complain. If he is working for extra sales that might mean a trip to Europe or a new piece of furniture, she is likely to become the sales manager's ally at home. The E. F. MacDonald Company, a pioneer in incentive prizes, sends out "teaser mailings" to the salesman's wife, urging her to "Cajole your husband, nag him." They send her a thimble and a note to "Give your husband the needle . . ."

A Sperry and Hutchinson Company advertisement

for its Incentive Division asks: "Do you know how to
motivate a salesman as well as his wife does?" The ad
goes on to say that when extra sales mean Green Stamps
for her, "She keeps after her husband to sell more, and
he *sells* more." According to S&H, one company that
used Green Stamp incentives doubled its sales every year
for five years.

Prizes are given not only to salesmen, but are occasionally given also to buyers. Marsteller, Inc., a New
York advertising agency, obtained notable success for its
clients by using substantial giveaways to get salesmen in to
hard-to-see buyers. The Clark Equipment Company, a
Marsteller client, is a large trailer manufacturer. There
were 300 big trailer buyers that were not Clark customers.
In order to get their salesman in to see them, Clark spent
$12,000 on a program designed by the agency. Each
buyer received in the mail a chef's hat and a Clark sales
message: "Clark salesmen wear many hats." This was
followed by a set of barbecue tools, a set of salt and
pepper shakers, a cookbook, a pair of padded gloves,
and an apron, each with a sales message. Last came the
salesman himself with a frozen two-pound steak and the
message: "This is the kind of personal service you always get from Clark." Operation Cookout brought in fifty
new accounts and $3,500,000 new sales. Other companies
have since made good use of this selling approach. Goodyear, according to Tim Colvin, who planned their programs, has become devoted to mail plus salesmen campaigns.

In addition to contest prizes and brass bands and
flashing lights at the sales meeting, another favorite device for making the salesman hustle is the *award*. The
award may come in the form of a salesman's club membership, a gold pin, a trophy, a letter from the company
president, or publicity in the company newspaper.
Oneida Silversmiths gives the Nosy Award: a silver cari-
cature of a salesman weighed down by two sample

cases, "his big nose upturned to focus on his 'nose for business.'"

The arguments for and against incentive awards go on continually. Bob Blashek is convinced that prizes and incentive awards are helpful to obtain specific short-range goals. He recalled that when he was a young salesman just out on the road, he had a line of paper tape among the many products he sold. The tape company announced a contest in which the salesman would receive credits toward any item in a home-merchandise catalogue in proportion to the amount of paper tape he sold. For a salesman who represented many lines this was an effective way of getting his attention. Blashek saw a truck loaded with cartons heavily wrapped with paper tape. He called on the company and sold what at first he thought was six rolls of his tape as a trial. When he wrote up the order, he realized the buyer meant six *cases* of paper tape. The company became a regular customer and a prodigious consumer of paper tape.

Distributors often resent and sometimes resist manufacturers who offer prizes and premiums directly to the distributor's salesmen, because this disrupts the distributor's control over his salesmen's effort. Salesmen may be tempted to devote an inordinate amount of time pushing less profitable lines in order to win a prize or a contest. The distributor may feel that a manufacturer should increase the sales commission if he has any extra money to promote his product. One distributor told *Marketing Management* magazine, "We don't like these bribes. . . ."[6]

It is an old problem. Back in the 1930s, a New York manufacturer sent its traveling men out to visit the homes of 500 store managers of large chains. The manager's wife was offered prizes if her husband's store sold a certain volume of Brand X. Meanwhile, the chain had invested heavily in a competing brand, and was unable to understand why it failed to sell, although it was cheaper than

Brand X. When the management discovered the secret appeal to the wives, they hit the ceiling.

A study of 169 industrial salesmen by Professor H. B. Kay questioned the validity of the sales contest on the grounds that it was eventually harmful to the salesman's motivation, "because if a salesman is motivated by the challenge of his work—as our study proved—focusing his attention on trips to Hawaii or award dinners sidetracks him. Do this often enough and you risk creating a sales force whose sole purpose for working is to win the next contest, whose members no longer enjoy the work itself, and who measure success in terms of gift certificates.

"Also, by setting up a sales contest, we are structuring a situation where there can be only one (or two or three) winners but as many losers as we have left on the sales force."[7]

A further objection was made to sales meetings attended by top salesmen from all over the country, held for the dual purpose of reward and training. "The poor slobs who need the training are back home plodding around their territories," remarked one sales trainer.[8]

The attitude of the salesman in the field toward the carrots dangled in front of him is, of course, as various as the human personality. The range encompasses a few cynics who see all motivational contests and prizes as manipulative and degrading to a few innocents who are wet-eyed with gratitude and eager to win. Most salesmen seem to regard extra nonmonetary compensation as desirable to a degree, depending on their own circumstances and the details of the specific incentive program. There is, however, one common response.

When prizes are offered, or quotas are set for sales within a given period of time, there is always the temptation on the part of the salesman to load up a customer with more goods than he needs. One company sponsored a contest for the most sales in the month of June, the prize being an expense-paid vacation for two. June sales set a record, but around November the cancellations began to come in. So many orders were canceled in November and December that the sales volume for those two months was a negative number. The sales manager ruefully remarked that he had rather have just given every man $1000.

At companies like IBM, where delivery schedules are long, often more than two years, a salesman with a yearly quota to meet will get a customer to order equipment and then cancel it after the first of the year. One former IBM salesman told me that during his first two years in his territory, he would never have made the 100 percent Club if he hadn't "watered the books." ("Water on the books" means that there is equipment on order that the salesman knows will be canceled.) However, there is a curious Parkinson-type law that might be stated thus: Once a company becomes involved in electronic data processing, it will find an increasing amount of data to process. Unless a salesman becomes a real water merchant, he can expect that much of the equipment ordered as a favor to him by a customer will never be canceled. By the time delivery is scheduled, the extra data-processing equipment will be really needed. Shel Eglash, former president of System Engineering Labs—a small rival to IBM—recalled that in his selling days at IBM, if he needed points at the end of the year to make the Club, he would select the piece of equipment with the longest delivery schedule and get a big customer to order it. He rarely had water returned.

Water, however, sometimes is returned, and at IBM a new salesman is responsible for all orders on the books after ninety days in his new territory. During those first months he will try to casually sound out customers who have equipment on order. Do they *really* need it? If they cancel after he has been on the job ninety days, the selling commission already paid to the previous salesmen is taken out of the new salesman's pocket.

In setting quotas for honorary clubs or special awards or prizes, most companies try to avoid water by accepting only noncancelable orders for credit.

The most interesting aspect of the fluctuating quota, and the parade of prizes, awards, and contests, is that the salesman's income is subject to radical change that is not always to his advantage.

A salaried employee is sure of his income. If he gets a raise, he keeps it. It is not withdrawn abruptly or renegotiated every year. He does not compete for it every month.

A salesman who works on commission or a mix of salary and bonus, will take at least a part of his income in special incentive awards. His earnings will not always reflect his effort or his volume. In fact, a salesman who does well this year is likely to find that his great success has convinced his company that they need another salesman in his territory. Next year, he will probably earn less money, or if he runs especially hard, he may even stay where he is.

Most salesmen find in the cheerleaders very little to cheer about. Or enthuse about.

Critics of the cheerleader approach to selling have long spoken out against demeaning the salesman and his work. In the early days of the Depression, a banker found the cheers fading. "I could not believe many real salesmen would stay permanently with a concern that treated its men like a lot of little boys. Salesmen of the 'whoop-la' sort may be quite efficient in boom times, but their enthusiasm usually evaporates when there is not much to be enthusiastic about."[9]

A more recent critic sounded off at the Sales Executives Club in New York. John McCarthy, president of a sales-training company, told the assembled sales managers that many companies treat their salesmen as if they were idiots. "Just picture them prancing through the hotel lobby dressed in ten-gallon hats and paper shirts and

boots! You can just see the other guests in the hotel pointing to the group and saying, 'Look at the salesmen.'

"This is the kind of inspirational hogwash that has no
place in selling today. The men feel like damned fools,
and you'll never see a lawyer or doctor treated that
way."[10]

Perhaps it is time to close the corporate kinder-
garten and concentrate on what one sales manager called
"the annual contest to keep your job."

Chapter Fifteen

Salesmanship by the Book

In 1870, there were only about a half million people involved in sales in the United States, but by 1900, the number had risen to two million, and at the start of World War II, there were seven million. As more and more salesmen were employed, the publication of books on salesmanship became a popular and profitable business.

In the enormous body of writing that has been produced on the subject of salesmanship, three broad categories are discernible.

The first might be called the practical, instructional approach, pioneered by Joseph Crane, an agent of the National Cash Register Company, who wrote the first sales primer in 1887. The book consisted entirely of a sales talk Crane wrote and memorized, including all the selling points he wanted to make during a presentation. When John Patterson heard about Crane's spiel, he got him to dictate it to a secretary and sent it straight to the printer. Thereafter, each Cash salesman was given

a copy of the resultant book and required to recite it
to Patterson personally when he visited the sales office.
It was as popular with the Cash salesmen as a numbered
canvas would be with a fine artist, but any salesman
reading this book today would feel certain that he could
have sold a cash register. Crane's book was a valuable
guide at NCR for years, and although Cash salesmen
no longer use a canned pitch, his basic approach is still
in use today.

Within a few years of the Crane primer, the sales
manual became the most serious literary effort in the
corporate world, producing such improbable, though typical, titles as *The Salesology of the Butterkist Popcorn
and Peanut Machine.*

During the 1920s and 1930s, a kind of generalized
sales manual appeared that gave advice and specific examples of selling tactics that had been used by salesmen
in a variety of fields. Selling strategy, once a closely
guarded secret, was now being openly discussed. One
book, for example, told about a refrigerator salesman who
had an egg delivered by messenger to each housewife
he intended to call on the next day. The housewife was
simply given the egg and requested to put it in her
icebox. When the salesman called at the house, he asked
to see the egg and then announced that it had not been
kept "safely cold." He was off on his refrigerator sales
talk before the housewife quite realized that she had
opened the door to a salesman.

When Crisco was being introduced, a canvasser
greeted the housewife at the door with a large can of the
stuff. As soon as she took it, he immediately took out
a pencil, which he held in his right hand, and a coupon,
which he held in his left. The woman was unable to
hand the Crisco back to the salesman and more or less
had to stand and listen to the sales talk, which began
immediately.

A more structured approach to selling was attempted

in the sales "textbook." Many books, however, that appeared to be straightforward practical books on selling turned out to be filled with platitudinous generalities, anecdotes, and sermonettes on hard work, self-confidence, and enthusiasm. The LaSalle Extension University books were major offenders on this score.

The A. W. Shaw Company was another publisher of books primarily intended as a home-study course to open the door of opportunity to all through an "exciting career" in selling. The company claimed in its advertisements to have sold 50,000 copies of a three-volume set called *The Knack of Selling*. The volume I read seemed designed to inspire the daydreams of idle clerks rather than to train salesmen.

In all the books in the sales-primer category, there was a certain cold-blooded cunning in regard to stalking and trapping a customer or "prospect" that people outside the sales business found insidious. Clarence Darrow, at the height of his career, took time to sample a few books currently being advertised, and his views were published in *American Mercury* in August 1925, a month after the Scopes trial had begun in Tennessee. "It is obvious," he wrote, "that these astounding books on salesmanship are symptomatic of the age. In literary quality, they are crude to the last degree. The motive back of all of them is not even veiled. The reader is simply urged to get the money and get it quickly . . . Alluring advertisements are sent broadcast to the struggling and dull-witted, asking them to part with their cash to buy books and take courses that may get money from others even more dull-witted than themselves."

There was no outcry from the general public, however—perhaps because few men were far enough removed from either the direct practice of salesmanship or the fruits of its guile to complain loudly about the ethics of the thing. And considering the similarities between a lawyer playing on the emotions of a jury and a salesman facing a buyer, I think Mr. Darrow might have exhibited too easy a conscience in condemning salesmanship by the book.

Others more involved with the subject objected to the upsurge of sales instruction during the 1920s for different reasons. J. R. Sprague aired his views in the *Saturday Evening Post* in 1929, taking a position typical of those whose sales experience harked back to the previous century of untutored drummers. "I have always been skeptical—perhaps unduly so—in regard to the experts who claim to be able to teach salesmanship in a few easy lessons. Perhaps certain fundamentals can be taught —but broadly speaking, salesmanship is a thing to be learned only by selling."

The second major category contained those books that generally espoused the "scientific" approach to selling and attempted to apply principles or "laws" to guide the salesman in understanding, and hence manipulating, customer behavior. The books on scientific salesmanship satisfied a need of the times when new inventions and discoveries constantly astounded the public and "What'll they think of next" was a common utterance, said with seriousness and fresh wonder. Salesmanship without a little psychology mixed in seemed rather old-fashioned by 1920. The salesman had always suffered from an occupational inferiority complex, and the scientific "experts" provided a little status to the business by suggesting that selling was more a function of the brain than the glands. In the preface to *Autosuggestion and Salesmanship* (1923), Frank Scott wrote: "Today salesmanship has attained the dignity of a profession, and the ablest psychologists and lecturers are engaged at high salaries to train young men for the important business of selling."

Publishers appeared with impressive names like the Auto-Science Institute and the Scientific Sales Society, whose books promised to reveal the "principles and se-

crets" of salesmanship—"advanced, modern salesmanship,"
that is.

It was E. St. Elmo Lewis, the advertising manager
of Burroughs Adding Machine Company, who had provided the "experts" with their most enduring formula, and
by the time most of them got to it there was nothing
new or modern about it. Lewis had illustrated his theory
of selling in 1898, at the age of twenty-six, with the
slogan, "Attract Attention, Maintain Interest, Create Desire." His basic idea has survived the years in many
forms. It appeared in an expanded version in *The Mind
of the Buyer* (1921) by Harry Dexter Kitson, a professor
of psychology at Indiana University. Professor Kitson
divided the sales situation into six stages: Attention, Interest, Desire, Confidence, Decision and Action, and Satisfaction. These elements constituted the "stream of
thought" in a sale, which the professor had the effrontery
to illustrate with a drawing of a "cross-section of a stream
of thought"—a large circle enclosing a lot of little circles—
an illustration worthy of Stephen Potter.

A better book, *Psychology in Personal Selling* (1926)
by Adolph J. Snow, defined the four steps of a sale as:

1. "The customer's wants, needs, desires, and his
   need for satisfying these."
2. "Securing conviction."
3. "Producing decision, secondary desire and buying
   action."
4. "Satisfaction of the customer."

St. Elmo's formula appeared in some form in almost
every book that attempted to analyze the successful sale.
In 1947 (and again in 1957) it emerged as *The Five
Great Rules of Selling* by Percy Whiting, Managing
Director of the Dale Carnegie Sales Course. The great
rules were concerned with attention, interest, conviction,
desire, and close.

The writer who did the most to make salesmanship

sound a little more profound than this was Charles Bennett, who described himself as "B.C.S., A.M., Ph.D., Sales Counselor and Director of the American Efficiency Bureau (whatever that was), formerly with the Department of Marketing of De Paul University and President of the Bennett Realty Corporation." He was the author of *Scientific Salesmanship* (1933), in which he examined the three current theories of selling and offered his own.

He acknowledged the contribution of St. Elmo Lewis and went on to examine the theory of appeal and response worked out by H. L. Hollingsworth and outlined in *Advertising and Selling* (1923), originally given as a series of talks before the Advertising Men's League in 1913. Professor Hollingsworth said that there were two basic ways of appealing to a prospect. The higher form of appeal—the long circuit—aimed at the rational side of man's nature. The short circuit—the emotional appeal— automatically created a response by the nature of the subject. Sales offerings of machine tools and perfume were aimed at different parts of the nervous system.

The third theory of sales was that of Edward K. Strong, Jr., set forth in his *Psychology of Selling and Advertising*. Selling effort should be directed toward man's "wants," he said, and attention and interest would follow as a matter of course. Some of man's wants, however, were "acquired" or artificially stimulated, a concept which Strong illustrated with the story of the piano salesman who built a large business among the poor working people after he had overheard a woman talking about how much she wanted her little Mary to be a lady. Henceforth, the salesman used "Make Mary a Lady" as his theme, instead of "Learn To Play a Piano."

Bennett's theory was based on what he called "the law of expansion of meaning," which said that "Every meaning of an object and its interpretation by an individual will conform to his value complexes." Value complexes, said Bennett, were "patterns of conscious socialized behavior."

There were four steps in his formula for making a sale, the first being an analysis of the customer's value complexes. The salesman presented the proposition (that is, the product or service he was selling) and explained its selling features. The salesman next had to explain the proposition according to the prospect's value complexes. Finally, he had to overcome the prospect's objections. There was no formal "close," since the sale would be consummated more or less naturally when the last customer objection had been laid to rest.

Today, when automobiles are routinely sold as sex objects, and when aluminum chloride, or some similar compound used in antiperspirants, is sold as a guarantee against social inferiority, the concept of "expansion of meaning" is undeniable. It is doubtful, however, that a salesman could determine a customer's value complexes with sufficient insight to expand the meaning in the desirable direction within the time of the brief encounter typical of most selling situations. At most, the salesman could talk in terms that the customer would understand and emphasize the features that he thought would appeal to the customer, which is what salesmen have always done, and if there was a difference between "expansion of meaning" and Mary's piano, I didn't discover what it was.

The third category of sales books were inspirational in nature and partly autobiographical. The advice on selling was built around the author's own personal experience.

Around the turn of the century, most of the books on salesmanship were reminiscences of traveling salesmen, or stories about them by retired buyers, hotel stenographers, and sales managers. Inspiration and encouragement were dispensed by trade magazines, beginning with *The Sample Case* in 1905, *Salesman's Magazine* in 1910, and *Salesmanship* in 1916.

Worthington C. Holman, who had spent two years in the sales and advertising department at NCR, wrote a

book in 1905 called *Ginger Talks,* which was a collection
of little speeches for a sales manager to deliver to his
lagging salesmen on such topics as courage, enthusiasm,
optimism, hope, and the thorough chewing of one's food,
the latter topic being one of John Patterson's obsessions.
The talks contained little practical information and re-
sembled the coach's half-time exhortations in the locker
room. One of the first books to establish the pattern
for the inspirational autobiography was *Men Who Sell
Things,* written in 1912 by Walter Moody, a former
traveling salesman, sales manager, and business book
editor for LaSalle Extension University.

Moody expressed the feeling that selling was a work
of high purpose, and a man approaching that work revealed his fineness or meanness of character by his success
or failure, overlooking the possibility that a salesman
could be both undeserving and successful. Salesmanship
was a religion, and a man entering it was expected to
follow the gospel—a "sales creed"—which Moody quoted
and which said in part:

> I believe in the goods I am selling, in the firm
> I am working for, and in my ability to get results.
>
> I believe that a man gets what he goes after; that
> one order today is worth two orders tomorrow; and
> that no man is down and out until he has lost faith
> in himself.
>
> I believe in today and in the work I am doing;
> in tomorrow when it comes, and in the work I hope
> to do; and in the sure reward which the future holds.
>
> I believe in courtesy, in generosity, in good cheer,
> in kindness, in friendship, and in honest competition.
>
> I believe there is an order somewhere for every
> man ready to take one. I believe I am ready right
> now.

This would seem an unnecessarily pious vow for
men out to sell suction pumps, hats, breakfast foods, and

other secular lines of goods and services, but the gospel of salesmanship being evolved was harsh in its demands on the individual, and salesmen seemed eager to believe that God wanted them to make their quotas.

Selling, according to the gospel, which Moody and others were beginning to preach, was an act that arose from—and was solely dependent upon—the inner resources of the salesman, a belief in harmony with the Protestant ethic of hard work and dedication. Each man was capable of achieving his own economic or spiritual salvation.

The study of economics, sociology, and psychology shows that many forces act upon the fate of the individual salesman, and his success or failure is not entirely of his own making, the gospel notwithstanding. (Sales executives then, as now, sought to understand these influences and make use of them, without, of course, relieving the salesman of his burden of accountability for making sales.) In none of the inspirational books did the idea appear, even briefly, that a lost sale was anybody's fault but the salesman's. One has the feeling that the salesmen who sold saddles, horseshoes, and wagons must have gone out of business thinking that the right sales argument—if they could only have found it—delivered with sufficient enthusiasm, would have overcome the customer's desire for an automobile.

The salesman's gospel allows for no excuses about territory, product, prices, hard times, or competition. Hard work, smart thinking, and faith in himself is all that is needed to survive and thrive. Failure is the indisputable evidence of some personal inadequacy, the root of which is laziness, and the symptom is usually a lack of enthusiasm about his product or himself.*

* A friend of mine who is a salesman said you could drop him naked into the desert, and he would drive back to New York in a Cadillac. Most salesmen, in their more ebullient moments, are capable of this high degree of self-confidence. Should he perish in that desert, he would hold himself accountable for his own demise, though he might complain loudly about the heat and lack of water.

This gospel was expressed in numerous books that appeared with great frequency since the age of marketing raised salesmanship from the drummer's pastime to a matter of economic necessity in the battle to keep consumption abreast of production. These writings are a neglected part of our cultural heritage and contain some of the best expressions of the Protestant ethic in its most practical form, adding a uniquely New World flavor to man's desire to control his own destiny.

The gospel books on salesmanship combined the American taste for emotional, inspiring lectures and sermons with the democratic belief that anything could be done by a free man of solid resolve. Good rousing speakers have always been in demand, whether they talked religion or business, and one of the most successful, in fact, talked about both. Russell H. Conwell was a Baptist minister who felt that it was a man's Christian duty to make money because of all the good it could do, pointing out to his appreciative audiences that it was not money but the *love* of money that was the root of all evil. He delivered his famous lecture "Acres of Diamonds" over 6000 times, and founded Temple University with the proceeds. His lecture was popular with groups of salesmen and with general audiences.

The notion that it was somehow a patriotic or deeply spiritual act to sell something was a theme of the gospel books, but expressions of this sentiment appeared in the general publications as well and became a well-worn part of American folklore, sharing an uncomfortable existence with the public's dislike for persistent salesmen.

An example of the adulation accorded to salesmen was an open letter printed in the *Saturday Evening Post* in answer to a little boy named Billy, who wrote, so they said, and asked "What is a salesman?"

The answer was a folksy description of the salesman as cultural hero. "What is a salesman? He's a lot of things, Billy. He's a front-office buck private . . . a general in the field.

"He's the fellow that feeds a thousand stomachs every day in the year—stomachs that belong to those who make and distribute the things he sells. But he seldom finds time to feed his own face at home with mom and the kids . . . Whether it be chewing gum or tractors, he sells—sells those things that make Americans American.

"Quotas to him are sales-convention handicaps that make the game fun. Others may work a forty-hour week. But the salesman kicks because there are not more hours in every day. He's the fellow that does while others don't. And he loves it! Let's hope he keeps on—for the sake of the life we enjoy in the U.S.A." Rare was the writer who saw salesmanship without these overtones of patriotism or religion.

Some writer-salesmen, however, added an element of sex to characterize the selling situation. Walter Burns, author of *How Six Selling Secrets Jumped My Income From $85 to $1100 a Week*, was a marine stationed in the Pacific during the Second World War. He spent his time daydreaming a little differently than most G.I.s. "One rainy night I was sloshing across camp—thinking about girls and selling . . . when the idea hit me. *Selling is like romancing a girl.*"

Burns equated making an appointment with a customer to getting a date with a girl, and closing a sale with getting a "kiss." (His customer's reaction to this bit of philosophy would have been interesting.) His six secrets weren't as racy as you might think, consisting of mostly routine sales advice plus some warmed-over St. Elmo Lewis.

A lot of men who went through the war came home to postwar jobs as salesmen, and they went to work with great energy, and—like Burns—they reaffirmed their faith in positive thinking, to use a phrase that made a career for Norman Vincent Peale. "A man who lacks confidence tends to crawl. A confident man thinks success and becomes a success," wrote Burns.

The fresh infusion of eager salesmen brought forth a new crop of sales books. Among the inspirational how-to's on the market to instruct and inspire the new men, the classic was Frank Bettger's *How I Raised Myself From Failure to Success in Selling*. Bettger was an insurance salesman and later a lecturer for Dale Carnegie, and his book became a Bible for hundreds of thousands of salesmen, who must have felt that they stood too close to failure for comfort. *How I Raised Myself*, as it is known in the trade, has sold over 400,000 copies and continues to sell 15,000 a year, according to the publisher.

There is a mythical character that has been created from such writings, and he is recognizable from book to book by his devotion to his job, his incredible zeal, his unquestioning acceptance of the inherent good of salesmanship, and his willingness to bend his own personality to the good of the sale.

This ideal salesman was expected to believe that nothing could stop him from making a sale. "You've got all you need to succeed in Selling, if you're reasonably sure that your intelligence is at least average and you are willing to work," wrote Leon Epstein in *Where To Go From No*.

"You can decide what you want your total monthly or annual income to be, and reach it.

"You can determine in advance just how many Big Sales you need to accomplish your personal objectives, and complete them," wrote Abbott Smith in *How To Get the Big Sales*.

"Believe within your heart you can reach your definite goal—and keep punching! Result—successful achievement," wrote Willy Gayle in *Power Selling*.

"*I believe if a man can maintain enthusiasm long enough, it will produce anything!*" wrote Bettger.

The salesman, fortified with such assurances, prepared himself to make the sale, only to discover, if he read on, that the sale was easily lost. In fact, it was so easily lost, the salesman must have wondered how he ever thought nothing could stop him.

"Unfortunately," wrote Leon Epstein, "a momentary lapse can bring collapse to years of painstaking effort. One slip can cost heavily. One neglected flaw can floor you."

"I got to thinking about the sales I had probably lost . . . ," wrote Frank Bettger. "Overtalking is one of the worst of all social faults."

"Don't try too hard . . . Don't be a pest . . . Don't talk too much . . . Don't overdo your gratitude," cautioned Abbott Smith.

"There's the way you shake hands, the way you stand, walk, and sit—in case you're offered a chair—whether you can hold off smoking until and unless you're invited to," wrote Ralph and Naomi Engelsman in *Keys to Modern Selling*.

"In Selling, careless talk or careless speech can lose the decision for you. . . . Clean-cut, articulate speech and a pleasing voice are as much a part of good grooming as imposing appearance," wrote Wallace K. Lewis, in *How To Make Yourself a Born Salesman*.

Did the salesman have an inferiority complex? Harness it, advised Elmer Wheeler, in *How To Put Yourself Across*. "Make it work overtime for you in getting you down the road to your daydreams."

Did he have some physical disability? "Glenn Cunningham, with feet scarred by boyhood burns, set track records. F.D.R. never let paralysis interfere with the carrying out of his duties as President of the United States. Bill Talbert became a tennis star in spite of disabling diabetes," wrote the Engelsmans.

Did he have personal problems? "Whether it was a strained marital situation, a feeling of being alone away from home and family, financial troubles, indictment of himself for missing sales, not being permitted to change his territory, the continued hot spell, death of his father, or a youngster in the hospital, every situation had a cause, and all were a common denominator in diagnosis of the effect—warped mental attitude which sapped up all selling effectiveness," wrote Raymond Lee in *The Mental Dynamics of Selling*.

The salesman was above such trivialities, but dwelt on a higher plane because he possessed the "power of imagination [which] has ruled the world since the dawn of history. Men like Alexander the Great, Napoleon, Leonardo da Vinci, Galileo, Darwin, and Shakespeare— down to the modern giants like Bell, Marconi, Ford, DeForest, and Oppenheimer—have exercised a power for good upon the world that must be carried on in ever-increasing degree by each succeeding generation." (What this had to do with sales is not clear, but such grand vague comparisons are frequent in sales literature.)

"To be helpful, imagination must be creative . . . The power and performance of imagination overcome all forms of competition. Salesmanship must be *saturated* with imagination," wrote Harry Simmons in *How To Develop Your Sales Ability*. Unfortunately, imagination is not a personal attribute easily acquired. Enthusiasm is usually the substitute.

"The salesman who is sincerely interested in self-improvement need not be afraid to treat himself objectively," wrote Leon Epstein.

"Fire yourself up," wrote Willy Gayle, "by affirming the *inner power* you possess. Don't kid around with yourself, *give yourself hell* in a positive way . . . *and really mean it!*"

Gayle and several other writers have talked about "power selling," but the term has never been clearly defined. Dr. Pierce Brooks talked about it in *How Power*

Selling Brought Me Success in Six Hours and called it "selling with your heart."

These few examples give a general idea of the content of the inspirational how-to. The reader who has not encountered similar examples will be a rare bird in America, where belief in the power of determined enthusiasm is drilled into our heads at an early age along with the multiplication tables and diagramed sentences. In fact, it might be said that our general lack of interest in the welfare of those less well off than ourselves stems partly from our belief that the poor just aren't trying hard enough.

The inspirational how-to book is not as popular now as it used to be, which may indicate the dawn of realism in wonderland. Paul Buralli at Prentice Hall—a big publisher in the field—said that sales books of this type "peaked out" in the early sixties in favor of organic cookbooks and the occult, but the market for books to inspire the sales force has not yet been drained. Lester Garrett, sales manager at Frederick Fell, Inc., reported brisk sales of *The Greatest Salesman in the World,* an unusual entry into the field. The greatest salesman is a character named Hafid who lived at the time of Christ. As a young and unsuccessful traveling salesman, whose line was robes, Hafid comes across the Holy Family living in a cave and gives one of his robes to the infant, thinking that "With care it should last a lifetime." Years later, Hafid—now the "greatest salesman in the world"—is approached by Paul, who carries the robe left behind by the risen Christ. Hafid examines the label and finds that it was made by the house he traveled for, and by Paul's description of the circumstances surrounding the birth, particularly the bright star, Hafid concludes that it is the robe he gave away. Paul, it seems, has been unsuccessful in "selling" the teachings of Christ, and is commanded by a voice to seek out the greatest salesman for advice. After all,

says the voice, "Even the word of God must be sold
to the people. . . ."

Hafid then reveals to Paul the secrets of salesmanship and saves Christianity. (Example of one of the
secrets: "I will persist until I succeed.") The revelation,
to readers of sales-success literature, is very old wine in
imitation antique bottles, but in the first two years *The
Greatest Salesman* sold over 110,000 copies, mostly in
bulk lots to companies for distribution among the salesmen.

It seems clear from an examination of books on salesmanship that as a group they are characterized by a
belief in the individual which might be more commenda-
ble were it not carried to the extreme. As it exists, the
gospel is a living satire of democratic values, shielded
from laughter and criticism by the pretense that salesmen are vital to the country's survival, a claim that could
be made with equal success by firemen, postmen, ma-
chine-tool operators, or garbage collectors. Selling is a
job like any other, necessary and important—or it wouldn't
exist—but inseparable from the whole, a fact that the
sales industry seems to feel must be concealed from itself.

Chapter Sixteen

The Endless Road

E. B. Weiss, in his book *The Vanishing Salesman*,[1] predicts that the number of salesmen in America will decline because of their increasing cost and declining usefulness. The salesmen who will do the vanishing are the "salesmen representing the major consumer-goods industries—food, drugs, soft goods, hard goods, and calling on store buyers and middle-rank retail and wholesale executives. . . ."[2] In twenty years, he expects the nation's sales force to be cut in half, a process he believes has already begun. While precise, up-to-the-minute figures are unavailable, American business planned in 1970 to spend over $6.5 billion on finding and training 1,082,-750 new sales people in spite of the fact that half of them will have left or been fired by the end of the second year. These figures are for the total sales work force employed by "manufacturing, wholesalers, retailers, utilities, transportation, banking, finance and service."[3] And according to *Agency Sales Magazine*, referring to industry salesmen,

employers will spend $978 million to locate and train 152,-
000 new salesmen.[4]

The high turnover rate among salesmen has long
been deplored as a major expense in every sales department, and every industry has figures on how much it
costs to hire and train a man, usually cited as somewhere
between $5000 and $6000, although one sales magazine
said it could cost as much as $35,000,[5] and it can be
even more expensive not to fire a salesman. In one
company with a hundred-man sales staff, the bottom
sixteen salesmen were "marginal" producers considered
by the sales analyst to represent a loss to the company
of the sum of their salaries ($206,224) plus the po-
tential business they should have gotten but did not.[6]

The cost of calling on the customer is now estimated at around $47 and is expected to rise to $100
by 1975. The current cost per call represents an increase
of 10 percent over 1968, when the cost was put at $28,
if you consider that the size of the average order has
also risen, from $6132 to $9199.

By various statistics, it is possible to document
the fact that salesmen are expensive. A survey of fifteen
major industries revealed that the cost of selling was
11.8 percent of the dollar volume, half of which was for
the salesman's commission, salary, and travel expenses.[7]

Mr. Weiss's contention that salesmen are expensive,
and getting more so, is true, but there is no evidence
that salesmen are becoming ectoplasmic. Other factors
which will, he feels, contribute to the decline in the
use of salesmen in the future are: the decline of the value
of personal selling, lack of enough talented salesmen
among the disaffected youth, resistance of wives to part-
time husbands, the unionization trend among salesmen,
the poor status of being a salesman, and "the frustrations
and inconveniences of travel."[8]

Weiss points out that 1000 corporations account for
70–90 percent of all business volume, and by 1980, the

number of such corporations will have fallen to 700. These companies tend to buy by committees that do not see salesmen. And they produce many of their own products. Sears, for example, does an annual volume of $10 billion. Its own factories produce $2 billion, and it "has financial interest in suppliers producing another $2 billion."[9] Not much room there for a salesman, even on orders to plants in which Sears has no interest. I met a buyer from Sears on a trip, who told me that once he bought a line, he didn't expect to pay a commission. He might on the first order, but on any repeat business, Sears wanted to deal directly with the factory, and "he wasn't about to pay any salesman a commission then." He cuts the price so close, the commission would have to be paid by the manufacturer at the expense of his own profit. Everyone wants to buy wholesale, and vanishing commissions lead quickly to vanishing salesmen. To the extent that manufacturing and retailing merge in the future, the salesman with a territory will suffer, but such may not be the case, as we will presently see.

The lack of interest in—or talent for—selling among the young may not diminish the number of salesmen. The disaffection of youth, in its present form, is transitory, although disaffection in some form seems to be a permanent feature of our society. A few years ago, a survey of college students revealed a unanimous aversion to sales as a career, yet enough students, upon graduation, became salesmen to avert any noticeable shortages.

Sales managers, as far back as there have been sales managers, have complained about the lack of sales talent. They still complain today—a study of one industry found that 83.9 percent found difficulty finding good sales people. A similar complaint in the future is to be expected.

When the need to earn a living arises, as it inevitably does, youth will take whatever jobs are available. True, little boys no longer dream of being traveling salesmen

as they did fifty or sixty years ago, but the salesman's
job has much to commend itself to youth, disaffected or
otherwise. The salesman, after all, has more freedom than
most working people. He is out of the office much of the
time and has control over his own schedule. While he
may have uncomfortable moments, he is at least not tied
to a desk and compelled to spend his working hours
under the watchful eye of his manager.

As for the wives, they have always been resistant
to long business trips, but since the introduction of jet
planes and—more importantly, since most salesmen travel
by car—the construction of the Interstate Highway System, many salesmen who used to be on the road all week
are now able to make it back home almost every night.
Travel is an accepted fact of life today and should not
contribute to the decline of the salesman.

The unionization of salesmen will be a factor for
future consideration as long as salesmen are supplied
with compelling reasons for organizing, such as the continual manipulation of their income—usually with the intent to pay the same wages for more sales—and the use
of humiliation as a management device. Leonard Boudin,
the lawyer who represented a group who organized the
Metropolitan Life Insurance Company agents, said:
". . . I found tired, harassed, middle-aged insurance
men being put in a corner with a dunce cap on their
head when they didn't sell their quota of policies. It
was feudal, and they had no recourse."[10] Such "motivational" tactics will certainly add to the union's appeal
and help overcome the resistance of white-collar workers
to organizing efforts.

The salesmen who would gain the most by either
unionizing or forming a stronger trade association are
the independent sales agents. At present they are working under contracts that can be canceled by the manufacturer without cause on thirty-days' notice. The frequent result of this arrangement is that a manufacturer

will use agents, who work on straight commission, to get a new product established. Once it begins to sell, he fires the agent and turns it over to a salaried salesman. The agent has thus done the unprofitable task of getting the product introduced in his territory, but he misses the payoff. At the agents' conventions and in their trade publications the inequities of the contract are the main topics, but the unionization of these agents seems unlikely. The agency is a small business, and the salesmen see themselves as being closer to business than labor. Then, too, they are reluctant to press the issue for fear of driving manufacturers to hire their own salesmen rather than submit to a binding contract, although there is strong sentiment among the agents for a law similar to Puerto Rico's P.L. 75, which made it illegal to fire an agent who performed according to certain defined standards.

As for poor status and the frustrations of travel, the former has not been very high for a long time, and the latter has never been less of a problem. Travel today is less frustrating, though, of course, not as comfortable as the railroads, during their best days, for those travelers who rode the main lines.

Of the reasons Weiss offers for the decline of the salesman, only one raises serious questions. The decline in the value of personal selling would surely cause a dwindling of the sales force. The future of the salesman will be determined by the direction taken by two basic trends in production and consumption patterns that are now clear. The first is toward more and bigger of what we have now—more mass production, mass selling, and mass consumption of products that are becoming more and more alike.

Most consumer goods are heavily advertised through mass media and then piled up in stores where customers buy according to price and convenience. Some real selling goes on to get products into the store, but once an item is established and well-advertised, the game is played directly between the advertising media and the public.

Basic appliances such as refrigerators are not sold to the public by salesmen, though, as William White pointed out in *Why People Buy*,[11] they were first sold back in the 1920s by door-to-door salesmen, until the refrigerator became regarded as a necessity. Now the consumer goes to the store to buy a refrigerator, and the choices over which the salesman has an influence have to do with which model the customer buys and whether or not she buys it from him.

The same was true of air conditioners, vacuum cleaners, telephones, automobiles, typewriters, cash registers, and dishwashers, whose basic usefulness and desirability had to be sold to the public before the product could be sold in quantity.* The stores are now filled with products once thought useless and now considered essential. Customers come in to buy them, and are so determined that they can usually overcome the innate indifference of the sales clerk. The wave of the future seems to be retail sales without salesmen.

The specter raised by Mr. Weiss of gray-faced buying committees, or worse, a computer linkup between the supplied and the chosen supplier, suggests that even at the industrial level the process of buying will be devoid of salesmen, who only get in the way by trying to lead the committee or the computer away from its pursuit of pure reason and add to the cost. One visualizes giant interlocking companies controlling the flow of goods from raw materials to the finished product on the shelf, supported by millions of consumers who have been per-

---

* Marketing men sometimes forget the past and talk about how you can only sell what people need. Sam White, a marketing executive at Liggett & Myers, told an audience: "Today, people are too smart, too well-educated, too skeptical and too well-informed. Forget it, no salesman can get along by inventing need."[12] It has been done in the past, it is done now, and the future will be no different.

suaded by mass advertising cleverly concocted from in-depth motivational studies, all in lockstep, marching over the fallen bodies of lesser corporate beings and their parasitic salesmen.

There is, however, another script. Production and consumption might move away from the monolithic pro-ducer-buyer-distributor to a more individual and varied marketplace.

If this happens, the role of the salesman will be quite different, and announcements of his passing will prove to be greatly exaggerated.

The present system of mass production was created to accommodate machines that did the same thing over and over. Each machine on the assembly production line performed its task in a set pattern and could be dis-tracted from its original purpose only by a considerable amount of retooling or adjusting. Products of such ma-chines were all alike, and stayed that way until the manufacturer was forced to make changes. The endur-ing example of this was Mr. Ford's automobiles, which came in one model and one color. By working within these limitations, he was able to develop the production procedures that brought the price of an automobile within the reach of almost everyone.

With the development of electronic technology, ma-chines no longer need perform repetitively. The prod-ucts they make need not be the same. An exhaustive analysis of automated-machine capability is beyond the scope of this book, but a few examples will serve to clarify the point.

The Ford assembly plant in Mahwah, New Jersey, looks more like a lane of rush-hour traffic. You do not see an endless line of identical cars, but a random selec-tion of models and colors, some two-door, some four-door, some red, some green, some with disc brakes, and some with power steering. The customer's order is en-tered on a punch card, which is fed into the computer.

From the vast inventory of parts, each specified item is plucked and routed down the lines which converge at a point, and another point, until out of this incredible jumble appears the car, finished to the customer's specifications.

The newer production lines are now beginning to be automated. I spent an afternoon recently watching a Unimate, one of the machines widely used in automated production. It can pick up an object, perform an intricate series of maneuvers, and return it to its original position with a repeatability of 1/50,000th of an inch. The machine can hold a number of different programs—and in future development, an infinite number—and switch programs with ease. Unimate-type robots, in conjunction with numerically controlled machine tools, could produce machined parts of completely different specifications on a production-line basis.

It is conceivable that production technology can be developed to a point where the customer will be able to design his own product, and that, in effect, every product may be custom-made with the same economy as mass-produced products.

Thoughts similar to these were expressed by Mr. Lester Wunderman, president of a leading marketing company, in *The New York Times*. Mr. Wunderman saw in the social upheavals a new humanism that would, among other things, express itself in a revulsion toward mass-produced products and would demand instead more customized products. "For in truth, what we see in America as a major new marketing opportunity is the rebirth of individualism and human responsiveness, which may well portend the death of mass production, mass distribution and mass communication as we have known them.

"It is obvious that mass marketing and retailing concepts cannot properly handle the vast number of product lines that our fragmented markets will require. The requirement for fast turnover, limited inventories and low personnel overhead will soon make current retailing methods obsolete, except for staples."[13]

That something is going wrong between the consumer and the producer has come to the attention of others, whose job it is to see that nothing goes wrong. Noting that 80 percent of all new products introduced each year fail in less than a year, Ted Angelus, president of his own marketing company, told the Sales Executive Club: "Perhaps we are experiencing a trend which makes new-product work increasingly difficult. There is a widening gulf between consumer and marketer which makes it difficult for us to understand what consumers really want . . . marketers are asked to put together new products for a young adult market whose music they can't dance to, whose clothes they cannot wear, whose personal grooming habits astound them, whose sex standards they cannot fully accept, and whose political and social views tend to threaten the very life styles the establishment marketer enjoys and is trying to protect."[14]

Perhaps the mistake lies in the assumption that one product will satisfy the millions. Perhaps new products fail because the scale is too grand, the need for huge volume out of step with the times. That television, as a mover of vast quantities of goods, is on a decline is a generally accepted fact today. That nothing is going to replace it has not yet come to everyone's attention.

The trend away from mass production to customized products is coming as sure as tomorrow. One finds this thought expressed frequently in the speeches and writings of businessmen. Leo Cherne, Executive Director of the Research Institute of America, said: "Manufacturers accustomed to mass production, look-alike products, will be making a variety of goods to meet a growing demand for real variety from the affluent consumer."[15] While it is not clear just what role the salesman will play in its development, it seems most likely that he will retain his classic vital function of bringing together the elements of production and distribution as he has done in the past. Styles and tastes are likely to change at a faster rate, and the customer will not be satisfied with the same standardized product. The company that does its buying by committee and by computer will do so at its own peril.

The outcome will be decided by what the public buys, and the public is no longer disposed to be led so placidly by the media. Samuel Butler wrote: "God will not have any human being know what will sell." We must wait and see.

The salesman will not vanish. In diversifications of the future, which promise to be geographical as well as aesthetic, he will not cease to travel his endless road.

Footnotes

CHAPTER ONE

1. Odell Shepard, *Pedlar's Progress,* 1937.
2. Penrose Scull, *From Peddlers to Merchant Princes,* 1967.
3. Richardson Wright, *Hawkers and Walkers in Early America,* 1927.
4. J. T. Adams, *New England in the Republic,* 1926.
5. *Ibid.*
6. J. R. Dolan, *The Yankee Peddlers of Early America,* 1964.
7. Norris Galpin Osborne, ed., *History of Connecticut,* Vol. 4, 1925.
8. *Ibid.*
9. Adams, *op. cit.*
10. Dolan, *op. cit.*
11. Lt. F. F. DeRoos, *Personal Narrative of Travels in the United States and Canada in 1826,* 1827.
12. Gerald Carson, *The Cornflake Crusade,* 1957.
13. Dolan, *op. cit.*
14. Adams, *op. cit.*
15. C. M. Andrews, *Colonial Folkways,* 1919.
16. *Ibid.*
17. Wright, *op. cit.*
18. Wright, *op. cit.*
19. Carl Crow, *The Great American Customer,* 1943.
20. Priscilla Carrington Kline, "New Light on the Yankee Peddler," *New England Quarterly,* Vol. XII, 1939.
21. Sylas Holbrook, *Sketches by a Traveler,* 1830.

CHAPTER TWO

1. Don Marquis, "My Memories of the Old Fashioned Drummer," *American Magazine* (February 1929).
2. Horace Porter, "Railway Passenger Travel," *Scribner's* (September 1888). (Reprinted by *Americana Review,* 1962.)
3. Theodore Dreiser, *Sister Carrie,* 1900.

4. Asa Green, *The Pearl Street Drummer*, 1834.

5. Gerald Carson, *The Old Country Store*, 1954.

6. *The System of Commercial Traveling in Europe and the United States*, 1869.

7. *Ibid.*

8. *Ibid.*

9. T. J. Carey, *The Knight of the Grip*, 1900.

10. Penrose Scull, *op. cit.*

11. Carson, *op. cit.*

12. Carson, *op. cit.*

13. Charles S. Plummer, *Leaves from a Drummer's Diary*, ca. 1900.

14. Howard Peak, *Ranger of Commerce*, 1929.

15. *The System of Commercial Traveling, op. cit.*

16. Porter, *op. cit.*

17. *Commercial Travelers Magazine*, 1911.

18. Rufus Jarman, *A Bed for the Night*, 1950.

19. *Ibid.*

20. Marquis, *op. cit.*

21. *Publishers' Weekly* (February 8, 1930).

22. Dr. Alexander F. Chamberlain, *Journal of Religious Psychology*, Vol. 6, 1913.

23. Earl T. Hayter, "Horticultural Humbuggery Among the Western Farmers, 1850–1890," *Indiana Magazine of History* (September 1947).

24. *Ibid.*

25. George Ade, *The County Chairman*, produced in New York, November 24, 1903, reprinted in *The Best Plays of 1899–1909*, 1944.

26. Walter Moody, *Men Who Sell Things*, 1912.

27. Herbert N. Casson, *Tips for the Traveling Salesman*, 1929.

28. Earl Lamar Denham, *For Traveling Salesmen Only*, 1932.

29. John T. Fresh, *Twenty Years on the Road*, 1884.

30. Frank Will Smith, *Beyond the Swivel Chair*, 1940.

31. E. P. Briggs, *Fifty Years on the Road*, 1911.

32. From a mimeographed letter by Archibald Trawick, lent to me by Mike Wolfe, his nephew.

33. From the diary of John Darr, lent to me by his son.

34. Casson, *op. cit.*

35. Carey, *op. cit.*

36. Marquis, *op. cit.*

37. Leo Gurko, *Heroes, Highbrows, and the Popular Mind*, 1953.

CHAPTER THREE

1. Sigmund Freud, *Jokes and Their Relation to the Unconscious*, trans. by James Strachey, 1960.
2. *New Drummers' Yarns*, 1905.
3. T. J. Carey, *The Knight of the Grip*, 1900.
4. Josiah Allen's wife, "How We Bought a Sewin' Machine and Organ," *The Wit and Humor of America*, Marshall P. Wilder, ed., Funk and Wagnalls, 1907, Vol. IV.
5. *Drummers' Yarns*, 1896
6. *Madison's Budget*, No. 14, 1911.
7. J. Mortimer Hall, *Anecdota Americana*, Series Two, 1934.
8. S. D. Mann, *The Sample Case* (December 1937).

Most of the jokes used for this chapter had multiple sources, having been borrowed, stolen, and altered. It was impossible to credit the original source in most cases. Readers interested in pursuing the subject further may consult the Joe Laurie collection on microfilm at the New York Public Library, Fifth Avenue and Forty-second Street.

I would like to express my appreciation to Mr. Joe Weiss for lending me his collection for research.

CHAPTER FOUR

1. T. J. Carey, *The Knight of the Grip*, 1900.
2. Samuel Crowther, *John H. Patterson, Pioneer in Industrial Welfare*, 1923.
3. *Ibid.*
4. *Think, A Biography of the Watsons and IBM*, 1969.
5. Crowther, *op. cit.*
6. Stanley Allyn, *My Half Century With NCR*, 1967.
7. *Ibid.*
8. Harriet Lummis Smith, "Her Prerogative," *Commercial Travelers Magazine*, 1911.

For additional material on John Patterson, see *Wherever Men Trade* by Issac F. Marcosson, 1945, and *The Sales Strategy of John H. Patterson* by Roy W. Johnson and Russell W. Lynch, 1932.

CHAPTER FIVE

1. William Maxwell in *Collier's* (September 5, 1914).
2. *Sales Management* (October 17, 1925).
3. *Printer's Ink* (January 7, 1926).

4. *Sales Management* (October 3, 1925).

5. *Ibid.*

6. *Printer's Ink* (February 18, 1926).

7. *New Republic* (June 10, 1931).

8. *Business Reports No. 1*, Indiana University Business School, 1939.

9. Charles W. Hoyt, "The Marketing Age," a series of articles in *Sales Management* (beginning January 8, 1927).

10. Stuart Chase, "Six Cylinder Ethics," reprinted in *Essays in Contemporary Civilization*, C. W. Thomas, ed., 1931.

11. E. J. Goodspeed, "The Age of Salesmanship," *Buying Happiness*, 1931.

12. J. R. Sprague, "On the Road," serialized in *Saturday Evening Post* (October 5–November 9, 1929).

13. Clare Elmer Griffin, *Sales Quota Systems*, 1928.

14. *New Republic* (June 10, 1931).

15. Sprague, *op. cit.*

16. George Dartnell, Special Report on Improved Quota Plans, 1917.

17. T. C. Rice-Wray in *Salesmanship Magazine* (December 1916).

18. *Ibid.*

19. George Dartnell, *Special Report: Methods in Use by 21 Concerns To Reduce Cost of Travel and Operating Salesmen*, 1917.

20. *Ibid.*

21. *Sales Management* (January 25, 1925).

22. John T. Flynn, "Graft in Business," *New Republic* (August 5, 1931).

23. *Ibid.*

24. Robert Ruxton, *The Selling Force and the Selling Farce*, 1916.

25. Penrose Scull, *op. cit.*

26. The Chicago *Tribune*, cited in *Commercial Travelers Magazine* (February 1927).

27. Helen Christine Bennett, "One Million Excluded Men," *The Nation* (October 3, 1934).

CHAPTER SIX

1. J. H. Macalman, President of the Boston Dealers Association, in *New England Magazine* (March 1910).

2. *Living Age* (September 17, 1910).

3. *Ibid.*
4. Roscoe Sheller, *Me and the Model T*, 1965.
5. "Motoring Conditions in the South," *Country Life* (January 1, 1912).
6. "Some Startling Facts about the Auto Industry," *Country Life* (January 15, 1911).
7. Arthur Guiterman in *Country Life* (January 15, 1911).
8. *Current Opinion* (October 1920).
9. *Printer's Ink* (July 8, 1927).
10. *Sales Management* (March 3, 1928).
11. Defense Transport Administration, *A Rental Automobile Survey* (May 1953)
12. George Dartnell, *Salesman's Auto Allowances and Up-keeping Practices With Suggestions for Using Automobiles To Increase Territory Size and Yield*, 1917.
13. *Ibid.*
14. *Ibid.*
15. Gerald Carson, *The Cornflake Crusade*, 1957.
16. *Sales Management* (November 10, 1970).

CHAPTER SEVEN

1. *American Business Manual*, Vol. 2, 1912.
2. *Sales Management* (February 1, 1940).
3. *Sales Management* (August 1, 1940).
4. Gibert Rigg, *The Sales Engineer*, 1928.
5. Bernard Lester, *Sales Engineering*, 1940.
6. E. Patrick McQuire, *Training Sales Engineers*, 1964.
7. Dr. Julius Klein addressing the *Conference on Advertising and Selling*, 1929.
8. McQuire, *op. cit.*
9. David Seltz, *Successful Industrial Selling*, 1958.
10. Robert C. Hill, *Industrial Marketing* (February 1946).

CHAPTER ELEVEN

1. Raymond Ries, *The American Salesman*, University of Illinois, 1959. Unpublished dissertation.
2. *Printer's Ink* (December 1927).
3. *Barrons* (June 9, 1958).
4. Door-to-Door Sales Regulation (Hearings Before the Consumer Subcommittee on Commerce, United States Senate, Ninetieth Congress, on S1599), U. S. Government Printing Office, Washington, D.C., 1968.
5. McGraw-Hill, *Why Do People Buy?* 1953.

6. Everitt R. Smith, *Harvard Business Review* (1926).

7. *The New York Times* (May 16, 1971).

8. *Door-to-Door* Hearings, *op. cit.*

9. *The New York Times* (April 2, 1971)

10. *Consumer Reports* (July 1967).

CHAPTER THIRTEEN

1. Grant Nablo, "The Value of Character and Ability Analysis in the Selection of Salesmen," *Salesmanship* (December 1916).

2. H. L. Hollingsworth, "Selection of Salesmen," *Salesmanship* (December 1916).

3. Elliott M. Goldwag, *A Survey on the Use of Psychological Tests in Selecting Salesmen,* National Sales Executives, New York, 1956.

4. D. Schwartz, *The Relation of the Salesman's Wife to the Selling Performance,* 1960.

5. O. A. Ohman, "Research on the Selection of Sales Personnel at Tremco Manufacturing," *American Marketing Association,* 1941.

6. Arthur F. Dodge, *Journal of Applied Psychology* (June 1938).

7. Marion Bills, "Field Salesman," *Handbook of Applied Psychology,* Vol. 1, 1950.

8. Goldwag, *op, cit.*

9. Douglas Bray and Richard J. Campbell, "Selection of Salesmen by Means of an Assessment Center," *Journal of Applied Psychology* (February 1968).

10. David Mayer and Herbert M. Greenberg, "What Makes a Good Salesman?" *Harvard Business Review* (July–August 1964).

11. F. P. Tobolski and W. A. Kerr, "Predictive Values of the Empathy Test in Automobile Salesmanship," *Journal of Applied Psychology* (October 1952).

12. F. W. Howton and B. Rosenberg, "Ideology and Self-Imagery in a Prototypic Occupation," *Social Research* (Autumn 1965).

13. Ronald Partridge Cloyd, *The Use of Biographical and Projective Data in Predicting Productivity of Business Machine Salesmen,* unpublished thesis, Purdue University, 1962.

14. W. A. Tonning, *How To Measure and Evaluate Salesmen's Performance,* 1964.

15. Clement Julian Nouri, *A Study of the Effect of Sales Effort on Sales Volume,* unpublished dissertation, University of Wisconsin, 1961.

16. Howton and Rosenberg, *op. cit.*

17. *News Front* (October 1966).
18. W. K. Kirchner and M. D. Dunnette, *Personnel,* Vol. 35, 1958.
19. D. A. Rodgers, "Personality of the Route Salesman in a Basic Industry," *Journal of Applied Psychology,* Vol. 43, 1959.
20. Stuart Chase, "Six Cylinder Ethics," from *Essays in Contemporary Civilization,* 1931.
21. H. D. Marshall, "Monopolistic Competition and Self-Alienation," *Political Science Quarterly* (September 1957).
22. *Office Products Dealer,* undated reprint.

CHAPTER FOURTEEN

1. J. C. Aspley, *Special Report: "Stunts" that Put Life into Sales Meetings,* Dartnell, 1927.
2. Aspley, *ibid.*
3. Huston McCready, *Salesman from the Sidelines,* 1923.
4. *Wall Street Journal* (October 13, 1970).
5. Alexander Lowen, *Love and Orgasm,* 1965.
6. *Marketing Management* (October 1966).
7. H. B. Kay in *Sales Management* (September 1, 1970).
8. *The Sales Executive* (March 10, 1970).
9. J. R. Sprague, *Saturday Evening Post* (October 10, 1932).
10. *The Sales Executive* (April 26, 1971).

CHAPTER SIXTEEN

1. McGraw-Hill, 1962.
2. *Advertising Age* (June 22, 1970).
3. *The Sales Executive* (May 19, 1970).
4. *Agency Sales Magazine* (February 1971).
5. *Ibid.*
6. *The Sales Executive* (January 20, 1970).
7. *The Sales Executive* (March 24, 1970).
8. *Advertising Age* (June 1, 1970).
9. *Ibid.*
10. *The New York Times* (November 14, 1971).
11. McGraw-Hill, 1953.
12. *The Sales Executive* (February 3, 1970).
13. *The New York Times* (June 27, 1971).
14. *The Sales Executive* (May 11, 1971).
15. *The Sales Executive* (January 27, 1970).